T0309207

Advances in
Economic Forecasting

Advances in Economic Forecasting

Matthew L. Higgins
Editor

2011

W.E. Upjohn Institute for Employment Research
Kalamazoo, Michigan

Library of Congress Cataloging-in-Publication Data

Advances in economic forecasting / Matthew L. Higgins, editor.
  p. cm.
  The papers in this volume were presented at the 2009–2010 Werner Sichel Lecture-seminar Series held at Western Michigan University.
  Includes bibliographical references and index.
  ISBN-13: 978-0-88099-383-8 (pbk. : alk. paper)
  ISBN-10: 0-88099-383-9 (pbk. : alk. paper)
  ISBN-13: 978-0-88099-384-5 (hardcover : alk. paper)
  ISBN-10: 0-88099-384-7 (hardcover : alk. paper)
  1. Economic forecasting. I. Higgins, Matthew L.
  HB3730.A484 2011
  330.01'12—dc23

2011044001

The facts presented in this study and the observations and viewpoints expressed are the sole responsibility of the authors. They do not necessarily represent positions of the W.E. Upjohn Institute for Employment Research.

Cover design by Alcorn Publication Design.
Index prepared by Diane Worden.
Printed in the United States of America.
Printed on recycled paper.

Contents

1
Advances in Economic Forecasting

Matthew L. Higgins
Western Michigan University

The six chapters that follow this introduction are based on lectures the authors gave at Western Michigan University as part of the 2009–2010 Werner Sichel Lecture Seminar Series, organized under the same title as the present volume. The lectures were given over an academic year during a time when the U.S. economy was just beginning to recover from the "Great Recession." The economics profession's inability to predict this catastrophe may have seemed like an inauspicious background for a lecture series on economic forecasting. However, the economic distress and surrounding uncertainty actually benefited the series because they heightened interest in the topic of economic forecasting. The question-and-answer sessions following each lecture revealed that some audience members had a healthy skepticism of economists' ability to ever predict the future course of the economy. I think, however, that each speaker's candid and realistic assessment of opportunities to improve economic forecasting left most attendees with some sense of optimism.

Several common recommendations emerge from the following six chapters for improving the reliability of economic forecasts. Authors Dean Croushore, Kajal Lahiri, and H.O. Stekler all emphasize that improvements in forecasting will require proper evaluation of the performance of forecasting methods, focusing particularly on the ability of methods to forecast in real time and predict turning points in major macro aggregates. David E. Rapach and Tae-Hwy Lee, in their chapters, argue that the abundance of economic data can be more efficiently exploited through model and forecast combination. Rapach, Lee, and coauthors Michael D. Bradley and Dennis W. Jansen each advocate using models that are adaptive and perform well in the presence of nonlinearity and structural change. Below, I briefly summarize each author's chapter to help direct the reader to these specific themes.

In the book's second chapter, Croushore addresses the complications that data revisions have on economic forecasts produced in real time. He begins by advocating the use of forecasts provided by the Survey of Professional Forecasters (SPF). He argues that these forecasts are unbiased and efficient over long time periods. This survey is made publicly available by the Federal Reserve Bank of Philadelphia in an easily accessible format. (Croushore provides the Web address for this.) Furthermore, because this survey can be easily matched to the real-time macroeconomic data also maintained by the Philadelphia Fed, the survey provides a good data set for studying the role of data revisions in the forecasting process.

Croushore asserts that many forecast evaluation studies are flawed because real-time forecasts are compared to ex post forecasts that are based on revised data that actual forecasters did not have access to. To the real-time forecaster, recognition of the possible magnitude of data revisions causes uncertainty about model inputs, structure, and coefficient values. Croushore's research indicates that all three factors can degrade the quality of forecasts. Based on his own work, and the work of others, Croushore suggests that attempts to explicitly incorporate the process of data revision into model construction have so far had limited success in improving the quality of economic forecasts.

To illustrate these issues, Croushore examines forecasts in the 1990s from the SPF. When compared to the 2001 vintage actual values, the forecasts of gross domestic product (GDP) growth were consistently too low, and forecasts of inflation and unemployment were consistently too high. Forecasters appeared to be slow to recognize the effect of high productivity growth in that decade. When the forecasts are compared to actual values observed in real time for the variables, the forecasts appear much better. This may explain why forecasters were slow to adapt their models to the surge in potential output. Croushore's chapter demonstrates that research on the role of data revisions in economic forecasts is at a very early stage and should prove to be productive in the coming years.

In the third chapter, Lahiri addresses the intriguing question of how far into the future forecasters can provide information about the growth of GDP. He uses a survey of forecasts of the annual growth rate of GDP for 18 countries in the Organisation for Economic Co-operation and Development (OECD), obtained from Consensus Economics Inc. The forecasts are monthly and begin at a 24-month horizon. For each country and forecast horizon, Lahiri calculates the Diebold-Kilian information statistic and Theil's U-statistic. Although there is variation across countries, he finds that the quality of the forecasts tends to continuously improve as the forecast horizon declines. For many countries, he finds a dramatic improvement in the information content of the forecasts beginning at about an 18-month horizon. This striking finding suggests that the current state of economic forecasting provides useful predictions only when the lead time is a year and a half or less.

Lahiri also examines the usefulness of the probability forecasts contained in the SPF to predict downturns in U.S. GDP at different horizons. These probability forecasts have been reported since 1968 but have been greatly underutilized by the profession. Lahiri first demonstrates how to use a receiver-operating-characteristic (ROC) curve to select a probability threshold for signaling the rare event of a downturn. Selecting an appropriate threshold, he reports hit/miss frequencies, Kuipers scores, and odds ratios for the implied predicted downturn. He finds that the probability forecast contains useful information for predicting GDP declines for up to two quarters ahead.

Rapach, in Chapter 4, proposes forecasting methods to deal with problems associated with forecasting regional and industry-level (RIL) variables. When forecasting such variables, an economist is confronted with a large number of potential aggregate and region/industry-specific predictor variables. In such a scenario, a traditional regression approach would tend to overfit the model, and the resulting model would likely forecast poorly out of sample. To operate in this data-rich environment, Rapach suggests forecasters consider three new methodologies: 1) bagging, 2) forecast combination, and 3) factor models. Bagging is a Monte Carlo technique that stabilizes the model selection of the traditional approach of choosing variables based on significant t-statistics. Forecast combination averages forecasts from separate autoregressive-distributed lag models using each candidate predictor. A factor model uses one model and a small number of aggregate input variables to forecast the cross section of RIL variables. A final forecast is obtained by averaging the forecasts from the three methods. Rapach cites research that shows such methods have been demonstrated to improve the forecasting of financial returns, another environment where a multitude of potential predictors exists.

To provide evidence that such methods improve forecasts of RIL variables, Rapach applies the methods to forecast quarterly employment growth in Michigan and Missouri from the end of the first quarter of 1990 to the end of the first quarter of 2010. He constructs forecasts using the three methods and 11 predictor variables. He finds that the three forecasts tend to outperform forecasts based on a simple autoregressive model and also tend to outperform those based on regression models that use each predictor separately. The best forecast, however, is obtained by averaging the bagging, forecast combination, and factor model forecasts. Seemingly, each method contributes some unique information for forecasting state-level employment growth.

Chapter 5 is based on a Sichel lecture delivered by Jansen, in which he summarized his paper (coauthored with Bradley) exploring the possibility of incorporating nonlinear structure to improve the forecasts of financial and real variables. The authors conduct an exercise to forecast monthly observations on the index of industrial production, the 10-year Treasury yield, and the excess return on Standard and Poor's stock index (the S&P 500). They focus on the threshold autoregressive (TAR), logistic smooth transition autoregressive (LSTAR), and exponential smooth transition autoregressive (ESTAR) models, which allow the structure of the model to depend on an observable state variable. They use lagged values of the series as the state variable. For the industrial production and stock returns series, they also introduce a "current depth of recession" variable, which is the difference between the current value of the series and its previous peak. This variable allows the series to have asymmetric dynamics, depending on whether the series is contracting or expanding.

Although Bradley and Jansen find strong evidence of nonlinearity in the estimation period, the performance of the forecasts based on the nonlinear models is mixed. Depending on the evaluation criterion used, some of the nonlinear models do outperform naive and simple autoregressive models. Formal tests for forecast improvement suggest that the nonlinear models marginally improve the quality of the forecasts of industrial production and excess stock returns. Bradley and Jansen's work demonstrates both the challenges and potential benefits of exploiting nonlinear structure.

Stekler, in Chapter 6, presents a survey of methods for evaluating macroeconomic forecasts. He begins by posing a list of questions that any evaluation strategy should answer. He briefly describes the common statistical measures that test for unbiasedness, efficiency, and performance relative to a benchmark. He then describes two new developments in forecast evaluation. First, he proposes a method for jointly evaluating the directional accuracy of forecasts of both output growth and inflation based on the predictive performance test of Pesaran and Timmermann. Second, he furnishes an innovative method for appraising a forecast based on the benefit to the user. To measure the benefit of forecasts produced by the Federal Reserve (the Fed), he proposes comparing two things: 1) the targeted federal funds rate from a Taylor rule that uses the Fed's forecasts of output and inflation and 2) the targeted federal funds rate from a Taylor rule that uses the actual values of output and inflation. He reports finding that the Fed's forecasting errors produce a 100-basis-point error in the targeted federal funds rate. Although this error seems large, it is much smaller than errors produced by naive forecasts.

Having described evaluation procedures, Stekler then examines actual forecasts of output growth and inflation. Summarizing the findings of his previous research on forecasts for the Group of Seven (G7) countries, he reports that the results are mixed but tend to suggest that forecasts do have systematic biases and informational inefficiencies. There is also only marginal evidence that the profession's forecasts have improved over time. Stekler suggests that the poor forecasting performance can be attributed to the inability to forecast recessions.

Stekler concludes by describing the evaluation of labor market forecasts. U.S. unemployment is countercyclical and is coincidental with the business cycle in expansions, but lags in contractions. He asserts that the use of nonlinear models to represent this asymmetry has had only limited success in forecasting unemployment. He proposes a new method for evaluating the Bureau of Labor Statistics (BLS) long-term forecast of employment by age/gender categories and for evaluating the Census Bureau forecast of population by state. He decomposes the category/state forecast errors into components: errors that result from forecasting the aggregate and those that result from forecasting the category/state share. He evaluates the share errors using a dissimilarity index. He finds some evidence that the BLS employment-share forecasts outperform a naive forecast, but that the Census Bureau population-share forecasts do not outperform a naive forecast.

In the final chapter, Chapter 7, Lee presents a survey of the methods to efficiently combine abundant economic data to produce an improved forecast of a particular variable. He considers scenarios where there are many input variables and possibly many forecasts of the variable of interest. When many input variables exist, he presents recently developed methods for reducing the data using principal components and then constructing a forecast using a factor model. When many forecasts exist, he describes advanced methods for optimally combining the forecasts. This now-well-developed theory has mainly focused on producing point forecasts. Lee demonstrates that these techniques can also be applied to quantile, density, interval, and binary forecasts.

To conclude, I would like to acknowledge some individuals who made the 2009–2010 lectures a success and a pleasure for me to host. First, I would to thank the six presenters for their enthusiastic and stimulating public lectures, which, again, formed the basis for the present volume. The long success of this lecture series has always depended on the quality of our speakers.

There are others who must be acknowledged as well. The W.E. Upjohn Institute for Employment Research provided financial support and made the publication of this volume possible. Connie Volenski's administrative skills made the organization of the lectures effortless for me, and I am greatly appreciative. Werner Sichel deserves special acknowledgement for initiating this lecture series nearly 50 years ago. His nurturing of this series over the many years has made an invaluable contribution to the WMU Economics Department. Finally, I would like to thank my wife, Shohreh Majin, and my son, Bakhtyar, for allowing me evenings away from home to contemplate the future of economic forecasting over late dinners with the presenters.

2
Real-Time Forecasting

Dean Croushore
University of Richmond and
Federal Reserve Bank of Philadelphia

This chapter will discuss real-time forecasting in a macroeconomic policy context. I will begin by talking about the Survey of Professional Forecasters (SPF), a survey of private-sector forecasters. Next, I will discuss research on real-time data analysis and its importance in forecasting. Finally, I will discuss real-time forecasting in the 1990s.

In a policy environment, such as the one I faced for 14 years at the Federal Reserve Bank of Philadelphia, you have three basic choices for developing forecasts in a real-time forecasting environment. One possibility, used by many policy analysts, is simply to rely on forecasts made by others, such as the consulting firm Macroeconomic Advisors. After all, forecasting firms devote considerable resources to forecasting, so why not trust their forecasts? An alternative is to look at surveys of forecasters, such as the SPF. This gives you a range of forecasts, and you can base your decisions on the median forecast, which is usually a better forecast than the forecast provided by any individual forecaster. The third possibility is to create your own forecasting model. This gives you the ability to tweak the forecast to your own needs and to specify your own baseline underlying the forecast. You can do some simple things such as I did at the Fed—for instance, forecasting GDP for the current quarter based on the employment data that are released early in the month. Or you can run time-series models of your own specification, which often hold their own against much larger, more sophisticated models. Or, you could buy a large-model forecasting software program, such as the one provided by Macroeconomic Advisors, and then modify some of its assumptions to your own liking to produce your own forecast based on its model structure. Unless you have many resources at your disposal, however, you probably do not want to produce a large-model forecast on your own. You are unlikely to do better

7

than others, and almost certain to produce much worse forecasts, unless you have a large number of economists working on it, such as the dozens that work on forecasting at the Federal Reserve Board.

The major concern that you should have about all these forecasting models is the role of judgment in the outcome of the forecasting exercise. The more you study forecasting, the more you realize how much impact judgment has—there is no such thing as a pure model forecast. First, there is judgment in determining what model to use. Second, there is judgment about the underlying key parameters of the model: how do you determine the natural rate of unemployment, or the growth rate of potential GDP, or the equilibrium real interest rate, which are generally not determined within a model? Those factors tend to drive the forecast much more than you might think.

THE SURVEY OF PROFESSIONAL FORECASTERS

My own involvement with forecasting began in 1990 with a research paper in which I wanted to get data on inflation expectations. I used a survey that was run by the American Statistical Association and the National Bureau of Economic Research (NBER) and was known as the Economic Outlook Survey. The survey contained much useful information, and I was impressed that the survey had begun in 1968 and was the longest quarterly survey of forecasters in existence. But shortly after using the survey myself, I read an announcement that the survey was folding because of lack of interest and because there was no organization that was willing to run it. As an economist at the Federal Reserve, I thought the survey was incredibly useful—it gave great insight into the expectations of the country's leading forecasters. I was determined that the survey should not die, and so I contacted Robert Allison of the NBER and Victor Zarnowitz of the University of Chicago about the possibility of the Federal Reserve Bank of Philadelphia taking over the survey. They were both enthusiastic about having an institution like the Fed running the survey, and so we took over, missing only one quarterly survey in the transition.

After taking over the survey, I, along with my coresearcher Leonard Mills, began to rehabilitate it. We renamed it the Survey of Professional

Forecasters. We increased the number of participants (the participant list was down to 13 forecasters when we took it over), tightened procedures for production of the survey results, and added questions to increase the value of the survey to researchers and to policymakers. Today, the survey is used to provide forecasts to policymakers before the meetings of the Federal Open Market Committee, as well as to provide a solid database of historical forecasts for usc by macroeconomic researchers. The Philadelphia Fed's Web site provides complete details on the survey's history and all the individual responses to each survey, as well as write-ups for each survey and both median and mean data across forecasters for each macroeconomic variable included in the survey.[1]

If people wish to use a forecast, or a survey of forecasts, for making decisions, they would like to feel confident that the survey provides valid forecasts. Hence, much research has been done on the accuracy of forecasts from surveys, including the SPF. Two standard tests of the accuracy of forecasts are tests of 1) unbiasedness (that forecast errors have a zero mean over long periods) and 2) efficiency (that forecast errors are uncorrelated with information known when the forecast was made). If forecasts are unbiased and efficient, then people are likely to find them useful. If forecasts are biased or inefficient, then it should be possible for someone to improve on the forecasts in real time.

SPF forecasts generally pass the tests of unbiasedness—forecasts are unbiased in long samples. However, over short periods, the forecasts might have persistent errors. Figure 2.1 provides an example of SPF forecasts of inflation (based on the GDP deflator) compared with the measure of the inflation rate that is released one month after the end of the quarter.[2] In the short run, the forecasts sometimes exhibit patterns in which forecast errors persist for some time. But, as I point out (Croushore 2010), forecasters adapt fairly quickly to structural changes in the economy that lead to short-run persistence of forecast errors, and before long the errors disappear. If the forecasts were perfectly accurate, all the points would lie on the 45-degree line in Figure 2.1. Although many points are off the 45-degree line, on average over the 35 years of data shown here, the plotted points lie fairly symmetrically around that line.

Most research also shows that the SPF forecasts pass tests for efficiency. However, there are exceptions. Some of the exceptions found in the literature are not valid because although they show that the forecast errors are correlated with another variable, they don't use the data that

Figure 2.1 SPF Forecasts versus One-Quarter-Later Actuals

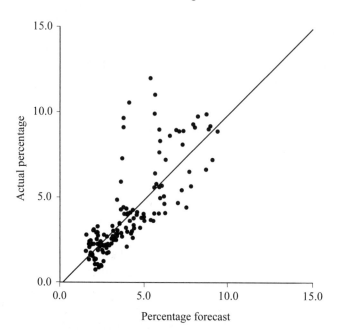

SOURCE: Author's calculations from data from the SPF and the Real-Time Data Set
  for Macroeconomists, Federal Reserve Bank of Philadelphia.

the forecasters had at the time they made their forecasts. Instead, those studies use revised data, which the forecasters would not have had, so their tests are not really tests of efficiency.

Ball and Croushore (2003) show that there is a tendency for forecast errors to be correlated with changes in monetary policy. As Figure 2.2 shows, SPF output forecast errors are negatively associated with changes in the real federal funds interest rate. When the Fed tightens monetary policy (and thus the real federal funds rate increases), forecasters reduce their forecasts for output growth, but not by enough. As a result, output growth falls more than the forecasters expect, and thus there is a negative relationship between output forecast errors and changes in the real federal funds rate.

For the most part, though, despite the Ball-Croushore findings, the forecast errors in the SPF tend to be small. The survey's forecasts are

Figure 2.2 Output Forecast Errors and Change in Real Federal Funds Rate

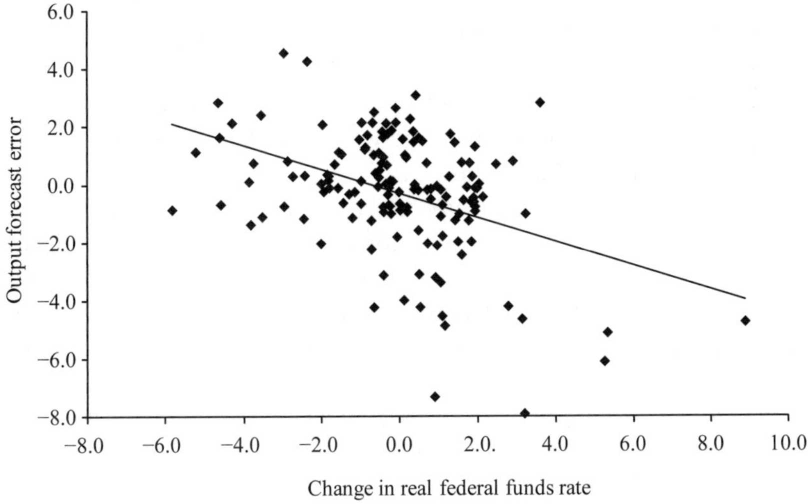

SOURCE: Author's calculations from data from the SPF, Federal Reserve Bank of Philadelphia; and the FRED database, Federal Reserve Bank of St. Louis.

generally better than simple univariate time series models at short horizons, as Stark (2010) notes in a recent review of the forecast accuracy of the SPF. However, there are some imperfections in the survey forecasts, especially for long horizons and with respect to the survey's efficiency in responding to changes in monetary policy.

REAL-TIME DATA

In evaluating forecasts of macroeconomic variables, researchers must be aware of data revisions. Some researchers are not careful about this issue, so they grab data from the current database and perform tests on forecasts as if the data in their database were the same as the data that were available to researchers in real time. This is a dangerous and invalid practice. Many papers have been written that show that some new model or other provides better forecasts than the SPF, but in most cases the forecasting advantage comes because the researcher is comparing forecasts from a model using a recent data set to forecasts made by the SPF forecasters using a completely different data set. Of course, the two sets of forecasts are not comparable.

To be able to compare forecasts made with a new model to the SPF forecasts in a legitimate manner, one would need to have at one's disposal a real-time database, showing what the data looked like at the time the SPF forecasters were making their forecasts. This is, in fact, the purpose of the Real-Time Data Set for Macroeconomists, which Tom Stark and I developed in the late 1990s and early 2000s. (See Croushore and Stark [2000, 2001] for details.) The data set was developed at the Federal Reserve Bank of Philadelphia, and new variables are continuously being added to the data set, based on work that continues at the Philadelphia Fed and work that my students have completed at the University of Richmond. A database of this nature needs good institutional support, as it is a public good. The Federal Reserve is a natural institution for supporting such projects, as it falls under the domain of providing macroeconomic data to the public for no charge.

Following the success of the Real-Time Data Set for Macroeconomists, other real-time databases have been developed all over the world. In the United States, the Federal Reserve Bank of St. Louis developed the ALFRED database, keeping successive vintages of the FRED (Federal Reserve Economic Data) database and making the data available in a convenient form. The Bureau of Economic Analysis has also, since 2002, kept all the vintages of its Excel files containing National Income and Product Accounts data and made that data available. The OECD now has a large real-time data set containing data for all the countries in the OECD, and the Euro Area Business Cycle Network recently made a real-time database available for all the countries in the Euro area. The United Kingdom, New Zealand, and Japan also maintain their own real-time databases.[3]

Some government statistical agencies in some countries have been reluctant to help researchers develop real-time data sets: they fear that if data revisions are examined by researchers, the statistical agencies will be subject to criticism because of systematic revisions. But research on data revisions is not intended to be critical of those agencies. The research findings might help the agencies strengthen their procedures to avoid having predictable revisions, for example. Economists understand that data agencies have limited resources and cannot produce perfect data releases given their constraints. The goal of research is to help people understand the limitations of the data and to explore the implications of those revisions for structural macroeconomic modeling, forecasting, and policy analysis. In addition, data revisions often reflect new information that cannot be known any earlier. For example, tax returns give the government statistical agencies much better data on income for the preceding year than the agencies had during that year, so GDP and income statistics are improved dramatically. Or, take the example of inflation measures: by construction, the consumer price index is not revised (except for changes in the seasonal pattern), whereas the personal consumption expenditures price index is revised; yet the latter is a much superior measure of inflation precisely because the revisions reflect changes in weights applied to different sectors that provide a more accurate view of the economy.

The typical structure of real-time data sets is shown in the data matrix in Table 2.1, which illustrates real-time data on real U.S. output. Each column reports a data vintage—that is, the date at which the data are observed. So, the column labeled "Nov. 1965" tells you what someone in November 1965 would have observed at the time. Each row shows the data for a date for which real output is measured. Thus the upper left value of 306.4 (in billions of real dollars) is the value for real output in the first quarter of 1947 as someone in November 1965 would have observed in the government's database. As you move across a given row in the table, you see how data are revised. For example, in November 1965, the first release of the data on real output for 1965Q3 was 609.1 (as before, in billions of real dollars). That number was revised to 613.0 in the data set of February 1966 and remained at that level in the data set of May 1966. The large increase seen in later vintages of the data of 3636.3 is not because of revisions to data but because of changes in the base year, from 1958 in the vintages of 1965 and 1966, to a base year of 2005 in vintages of 2009 and 2010. Moving down the main diagonal of the table, we see that the last recorded observation in each column shows the initial release of the data for each date: 609.1 for 1965Q3, 621.7 for 1965Q4, 633.8 for 1966Q1, 13,014.0 for 2009Q3, 13,155.0 for 2009Q4, and 13,254.7 for 2010Q1.

Table 2.1 Data Matrix for Real U.S. Output (billions of real dollars)

Vintage	Nov. 1965	Feb. 1966	May 1966	Nov. 2009	Feb. 2010	May 2010
Quarter						
1947Q1	306.4	306.4	306.4	1,772.2	1,772.2	1,772.2
1947Q2	309.0	309.0	309.0	1,769.5	1,769.5	1,769.5
1947Q3	309.6	309.6	309.6	1,768.0	1,768.0	1,768.0
1965Q3	609.1	613.0	613.0	3,636.3	3,636.3	3,636.3
1965Q4		621.7	624.4	3,724.0	3,724.0	3,724.0
1966Q1			633.8	3,815.4	3,815.4	3,815.4
2009Q2				12,901.5	12,901.5	12,901.5
2009Q3				13,014.0	12,973.0	12,973.0
2009Q4					13,155.0	13,149.5
2010Q1						13,254.7

SOURCE: Real-Time Data Set for Macroeconomists, Federal Reserve Bank of Philadelphia.

If data revisions were small and random, we would not worry about them affecting the structural modeling, forecasting, and policy analysis. But a look at the revisions should convince you that the revisions may be large and consequential. For example, Figure 2.3 shows the revisions to real output growth for the first quarter of 1977. From the data set's initial release at 5.2 percent, it was revised upward a few months later to 7.5 percent, and ultimately was revised upward as high as 9.6 percent. But later it was revised down as low as 4.7 percent in the benchmark revision of July 2010. So the revisions can be large and can occur even three decades after the first release of the data for a particular date.

You might think that such large revisions are rare and affect output growth for just one quarter, but even in the long run, data revisions can be large. For instance, if you average real output growth over five-year periods, you will find large revisions, which could potentially affect your view of long-run economic growth. As Table 2.2 shows, however, the five-year growth rate can be revised by as much as 0.6 percentage points, which is a large revision for a growth rate that is as low as 1.9 percent. For example, the growth rate in the first half of the 1970s was initially released as 2.1 percent, but by 1999 it was revised upward to 2.6 percent, nearly a 25 percent increase.

Figure 2.3 Real Output Growth for 1977, Quarter 1 (as viewed from the perspective of 133 different vintages)

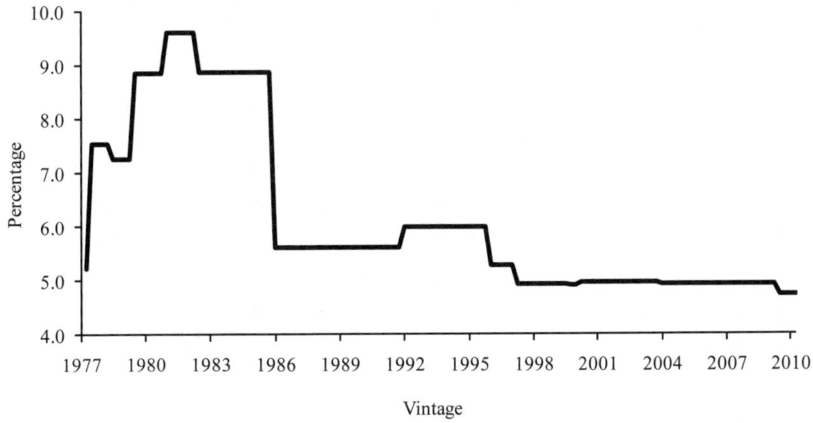

SOURCE: Real-Time Data Set for Macroeconomists, Federal Reserve Bank of Philadelphia.

In modeling data revisions, a key question for which an answer is needed for modeling or forecasting is whether the data revisions can be modeled as providing news or reducing noise. Data revisions that provide news are those that come about when the government's data releases are optimal forecasts of later releases. Under that situation, data revisions will not be predictable in advance from data known (by anyone) at the time the data are released. Providing such data revisions requires the government statistical agency to not report its sample information alone, but to use judgment and forecasting models to optimally forecast the values of missing data, so that the data release is an optimal forecast of later data releases. However, often data releases are not constructed in this manner, but rather fill in the missing source data with forecasts in such a way that the data release is not an optimal forecast of later data releases—usually because today's data release is correlated with other data known at the time. In such a situation, future data revisions will be predictable, and data revisions reduce measurement error, but each data release is not an optimal forecast of future data releases. For example, we know that there is a strong correlation between GDP data and employment data. If the government reports the GDP data

Table 2.2   Five-Year Average Annual Growth Rate of Real Output across Vintages

Vintage	1975	1980	1985	1991	1995	1999	2003	2009	2010
Five-year period									
'49Q4 to '54Q4	5.2	5.1	5.1	5.5	5.5	5.3	5.3	5.3	5.3
'54Q4 to '59Q4	2.9	3.0	3.0	2.7	2.7	3.2	3.2	3.2	3.2
'59Q4 to '64Q4	4.1	4.0	4.0	3.9	4.0	4.2	4.2	4.3	4.3
'64Q4 to '69Q4	4.3	4.0	4.1	4.0	4.0	4.4	4.4	4.4	4.4
'69Q4 to '74Q4	2.1	2.2	2.5	2.1	2.3	2.6	2.6	2.6	2.6
'74Q4 to '79Q4		3.7	3.9	3.5	3.4	3.9	4.0	3.9	3.9
'79Q4 to '84Q4			2.2	2.0	1.9	2.2	2.5	2.5	2.5
'84Q4 to '89Q4				3.2	3.0	3.2	3.5	3.6	3.5
'89Q4 to '94Q4					2.3	1.9	2.4	2.5	2.5
'94Q4 to '99Q4							3.9	4.0	4.1
'99Q4 to '04Q4								2.2	2.4
'04Q4 to '09Q4									1.2

SOURCE: Author's calculations from Real-Time Data Set for Macroeconomists, Federal Reserve Bank of Philadelphia.

based on its sample of the elements of GDP but ignores the information contained in the employment data, then its data release will contain measurement error, and data revisions will reduce noise. If I were a forecaster interested in predicting future data revisions, I would look at the data on employment and form a forecast of future GDP releases using a model combining the data from the GDP release and the data from the employment release. Such a forecast would be a better forecast of future releases of GDP than the government's release of GDP data.

This discussion raises a key question: should the government use the limited source data that it knows, combined with other information such as data on employment and industrial production, to form an optimal forecast of GDP? Or should the government follow a simple rule to fill in its missing data on forecasts of GDP and produce a noisy measure, ignoring data on other variables? You might think that the first method would be preferable, which seems intuitively clear. But the danger is that once you start forecasting with extraneous variables, since forecasting is more of an art than a science, the data releases for GDP will become very subjective. As an employee of a government statistical agency, you then open yourself up to the criticism that you are manipulating the data for political means. On the other hand, if you follow standard and well-established procedures for filling in missing data, you avoid any possibility of people thinking that you are manipulating the data for political reasons, because anyone can replicate your results, even though your data releases are not optimal forecasts of later data releases. In this situation, noise trumps news.

FORECASTING

How does a forecaster produce optimal forecasts in real time? First, any forecaster needs good data; a forecast is only as good as the data used to generate the forecast. The literature on forecasting mainly focuses on model development—trying to build a better forecasting model, especially comparing forecasts from a new model to other models or to forecasts made in real time.[4]

The first question in this literature is, "Are data revisions large enough to affect forecasts in a meaningful way?" We have seen that data revisions may be substantial, but what is the impact of those revisions on forecasts? Stark and Croushore (2002) suggest three ways this can occur: 1) by changing the data that are input into a model; 2) by changing the coefficient estimates of the model; and 3) by changing the structure of a model, such as changing the number of lags that provide the model's best fit. Stark and Croushore (2002) illustrate these ideas using repeated observation forecasting (ROF), which uses different real-time data vintages for the same sample period to see how forecasts change as the vintage of the data changes. By running these ROFs allowing changes in the lags in the model, allowing coefficient estimates to change, and changing vintages, we can observe all three ways in which forecasts change. To isolate which reason is the main cause of changes in the forecasts, we can run another set of ROFs that keeps the number of lags unchanged. A comparison of the baseline result and this one reveals the importance of changes in the lag structure in the model. To isolate the effect of changes in parameter estimates, we can keep the parameter estimates fixed and generate forecasts based on the different vintages of data, to see how much the forecasts are affected by parameter changes. Everything else must be due to changes in the data input into the model. Looking at the literature on forecasting with real-time data reveals no broad, general tendency. For some variables and for some forecasting methods, the forecasts change significantly because of data revisions. However, other variables and forecasting methods are more robust to data revisions, as Croushore (forthcoming) shows.

Because data revisions have mixed effects on forecasts, we might ask, "Is there an optimal method for forecasters to adjust their forecasts in the face of data uncertainty?" This is a much more difficult question to answer, and there have not been very many research papers that have tried to tackle it. A few papers seem to find some degree of ability to improve forecasts by accounting for data revisions (see Koenig, Dolmas, and Piger 2003), but the predictability of data revisions is fairly small, and larger forecasting gains may be found by pursuing aspects of modeling other than modeling data revisions. Some researchers model data revisions with time-series models, but the evidence in Croushore and Stark (2001) suggests that this will be problematic because benchmark revisions cannot be characterized as autoregressive moving average (ARMA) models, and benchmark revisions are the most significant type of data revisions. This explains why sophisticated filtering methods and state-space models often fail to deliver improvements in forecasts.

In summary, forecasters face difficult issues in forecasting in real time in the face of data revisions. It is not clear that the payoff to optimally handling data revisions exceeds the benefits of working on other aspects of forecast modeling, especially if data revisions are difficult to predict, as is generally the case.

APPLICATION: FORECASTING IN THE 1990s

To illustrate real-time forecasting problems, I will demonstrate with a real-life example from my own forecasting experience at the Federal Reserve. This example uses forecasts from the SPF to show the effects of data revisions. In the 1990s, the tech boom provided an unexpected burst of productivity, increasing output growth, reducing the unemployment rate, and causing forecasters to rethink key aspects of their models. In this section, I will look at the forecast errors made in the 1990s and show how forecasters eventually caught up to the change in productivity growth, although it took some time.

In my analysis, I will look at one-year-ahead forecasts of various macroeconomic variables. Each of the SPF forecasts is made in the middle of the quarter, shortly after the first release of the GDP data for the previous quarter. After that, data revisions occur once a year for data over the past three years, and benchmark revisions every five years or so cause significant data revisions for many years' worth of data.

Forecasts for real GDP growth made in the mid-1990s were wrong for many years in a row (Figure 2.4). The forecasters had expected real GDP growth to be just a bit over 2 percent for those years, and it turned out to be double that number. Forecasters were slow to realize that the tech boom had brought a persistently high growth rate of productivity, which translated directly into higher GDP growth. After persistent forecast errors from 1996 to 1998, the forecasters began to raise their forecasts for GDP growth in 2000. By 2001, the forecasts called for GDP growth close to 3 percent, just in time for the tech bubble to burst, driving GDP growth substantially lower as the United States experienced a mild recession.

With GDP growth occurring much faster than the forecasters expected, you might think that inflation would be higher than the forecasters thought, but in fact the opposite was true (Figure 2.5). Because the source of the increase in GDP growth was productivity growth, this was a classic supply shock, causing faster real GDP growth and slower growth of the price level. So the forecasters were again persistently incorrect in their inflation forecasts from the early 1990s until the end of 1999. They thought that output was above potential output, so they kept thinking that inflation would rise in the future. But in fact the forecasters had pegged potential output too low, and inflation fell almost continuously throughout the decade.

For the most part, the forecast errors on real GDP growth translated into errors in unemployment forecasts (Figure 2.6). The stronger-than-anticipated growth of GDP meant that the unemployment rate would decline more than was forecast, to be sure. But the forecasters were also very unsure of what the natural rate of unemployment was. Several years after the economic recovery from the 1990–1991 recession, they thought the unemployment rate might have bottomed out at 5.5 percent. But the tech boom kept the demand for workers growing throughout

Figure 2.4 Real GDP Growth Forecasts and Actuals

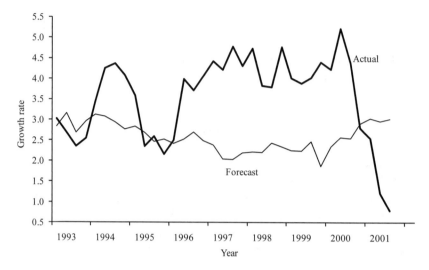

SOURCE: SPF, Federal Reserve Bank of Philadelphia; and FRED database, Federal Reserve Bank of St. Louis.

Figure 2.5 Inflation (GDP Price Index) Forecasts and Actuals

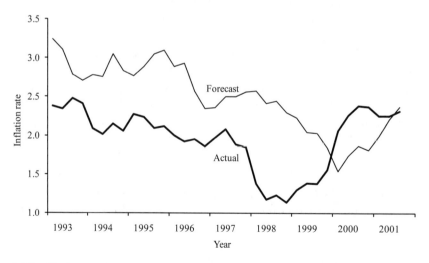

SOURCE: SPF, Federal Reserve Bank of Philadelphia; and FRED database, Federal Reserve Bank of St. Louis.

the decade, and the forecasters were wrong almost continuously that decade. They gradually ratcheted down their view of the natural rate of unemployment, but they were always behind the curve until the 2001 recession.

In describing these forecast errors, I have used a data set of vintage November 2001, which could be deceptive because of data revisions. In real time, the forecasters did not see the line labeled "Actual" that I have shown in these charts. Rather, they observed early releases of the data, which may have looked quite different. So, the forecasts in Figures 2.4, 2.5, and 2.6 look pretty bad, as they clearly made severe and persistent errors. But, if you knew only what the forecasters knew at the time they made their forecasts, the forecast errors would not have looked as bad, which is why the forecasters were slow to adjust their methods. For example, Figure 2.7 shows the same data as Figure 2.4 for real GDP growth forecasts but adds in a line labeled "Real-time actual" showing at each date what the last data point looked like when the forecasters made their forecasts. Of course, because these are one-year-ahead forecasts, the forecasters are always a year behind, so they still appear to make persistent forecast errors. But the "Real-time actual" line is

Figure 2.6 Unemployment Rate Forecasts and Actuals

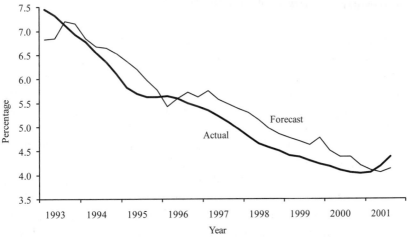

SOURCE: SPF, Federal Reserve Bank of Philadelphia; and FRED database, Federal Reserve Bank of St. Louis.

generally closer to the forecast line than is the "Actual" line. The point is, of course, that the forecasters did not know how severe their forecast errors were in real time; they only realized it much later.

Another way to see how slow the forecasters were to change their outlook is in their long-term forecasts for real output growth. The SPF forecasters are asked to provide a forecast for average real GDP growth for the next 10 years. As Figure 2.8 shows, the forecasters seemed to be reluctant to change their views about real GDP growth in the future, despite persistent real GDP growth rates of about 4 percent throughout the second half of the 1990s. In fact, the forecasters had lowered their forecasts of real GDP growth over the coming decade in 1996, just as the productivity boom was starting. They finally changed their view in 2000 and 2001, just as a mild recession was beginning.

CONCLUSION

Forecasters face a difficult task in real time. As we have seen, data revisions can wreak havoc with forecasts. As the example from the 1990s shows, when structural change occurs in the economy, it may take forecasters a long time to adjust their models. That situation is exacerbated when data are revised and the initial releases of the data are much different from the later data, as was the case with real GDP growth in the second half of the 1990s. The key to good forecasting is probably the use of judgment, rather than technical expertise. In the 1990s, some forecasters recognized the permanent (or at least persistent) shift in productivity growth, including Fed chairman Alan Greenspan. The SPF forecasts took a long time to catch up to the productivity boom, but some individual forecasters performed much better.

If you want to become a real-time forecaster, you should think about major elements of your model, such as the growth rate of potential output (and the growth rate of productivity) and the natural rate of unemployment. If you can make a better guess about changes in these variables over time, you can outperform forecasters who have greater technical expertise. But every forecaster, no matter how talented, will have trouble dealing with data revisions, which are largely unforecastable, and which can make forecast errors surprisingly large.

Figure 2.7 Real GDP Growth Forecasts and Real-Time Actuals

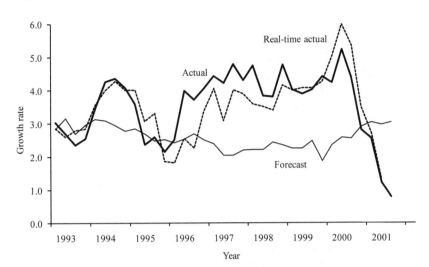

SOURCE: SPF, Federal Reserve Bank of Philadelphia; and FRED database, Federal Reserve Bank of St. Louis.

Figure 2.8 Real GDP: 10-Year Forecasts

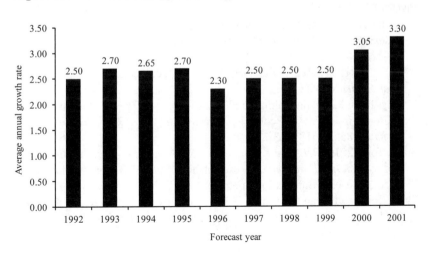

SOURCE: SPF, Federal Reserve Bank of Philadelphia.

Notes

1. http://www.philadelphiafed.org/research-and-data/real-time-center/survey-of-professional-forecasters/ (accessed January 21, 2011).
2. See Croushore (2010) for more details on the data shown here.
3. See my Web page at https://facultystaff.richmond.edu/~dcrousho/data.htm for links to all of these data sets.
4. In this section, I will report the main results in two survey papers, Croushore (2006) and Croushore (forthcoming).

References

Ball, Laurence, and Dean Croushore. 2003. "Expectations and the Effects of Monetary Policy." *Journal of Money, Credit, and Banking* 35(4): 473–484.

Croushore, Dean. 2006. "Forecasting with Real-Time Macroeconomic Data." In *Handbook of Economic Forecasting*, Vol. 1, Graham Elliott, Clive W.J. Granger, and Allan Timmermann, eds. Amsterdam: North-Holland, pp. 961–982.

———. 2010. "An Evaluation of Inflation Forecasts from Surveys Using Real-Time Data." *B.E. Journal of Macroeconomics* 10(1): Article 10.

———. Forthcoming. "Forecasting with Real-Time Data Vintages." In *Oxford Handbook of Economic Forecasting*, Michael P. Clements and David F. Hendry, eds. Oxford: Oxford University Press.

Croushore, Dean, and Tom Stark. 2000. "A Funny Thing Happened on the Way to the Data Bank: A Real-Time Data Set for Macroeconomists." *Federal Reserve Bank of Philadelphia Business Review* 26(September/October): 15–27.

———. 2001. "A Real-Time Data Set for Macroeconomists." *Journal of Econometrics* 105(1): 111–130.

Koenig, Evan F., Sheila Dolmas, and Jeremy Piger. 2003. "The Use and Abuse of Real-Time Data in Economic Forecasting." *Review of Economics and Statistics* 85(3): 618–628.

Stark, Tom. 2010. *Realistic Evaluation of Real-Time Forecasts in the Survey of Professional Forecasters*. Research Rap Special Report. Philadelphia: Federal Reserve Bank of Philadelphia.

Stark, Tom, and Dean Croushore. 2002. "Forecasting with a Real-Time Data Set for Macroeconomists." *Journal of Macroeconomics* 24(4): 507–531.

3
Limits to Economic Forecasting

Kajal Lahiri

University at Albany, State University of New York

Economic forecasting is not a very reputable profession. There is skepticism not only by laymen but by most academic economists regarding the true capability of macroeconomic forecasters. The conventional wisdom is that economic forecasters are mere charlatans.

However, there are numerous reasons why economic forecasts are so hard to get right. Not only do we not understand the continuously changing economic processes that generate the variable we want to predict, but we do not always have the appropriate measurements to identify the effects of sudden structural breaks that are due to economic and noneconomic factors. One way to make forecasts more useful—though not necessarily more accurate—might be to follow the "truth in labeling" often used in the marketing of many products. By this I mean every forecast should come with the associate expected errors like forecast uncertainty, so that both the forecasters and their clients would know what level of confidence to place in a forecast. This aspect of any forecast should be communicated, in addition to the forecasts themselves. Makridakis, Hogarth, and Gaba (2009) forcefully make the point that not having a proper estimate of the underlying uncertainty means succumbing to the illusion of control and experiencing surprises, often with negative consequences. It is in this spirit that since the mid-1990s the Bank of England and Sveriges Riksbank of Sweden have been reporting fan charts that show subjective confidence bands surrounding official forecasts. Since November 2007, each member of the U.S. Federal Open Market Committee (FOMC) has also been publishing information about uncertainty associated with that committee's economic outlooks. As Granger (1996) points out, in many disciplines there seem to be horizons beyond which useful forecasting is not possible; for instance, in weather forecasting it is four or five days. An essential element of forecasting is to extract useful signals from noisy data, and to project them into the future. Certainly, an aspect that provides limits to how far ahead one can forecast is when the forecastable signals get lost in the noise. It would also be helpful to be aware of these kinds of limits to economic forecasting in cases where the underlying uncertainty is hopelessly high.

Against this backdrop, in this chapter I will evaluate the capability of a large number of professional forecasters to forecast real GDP growth at different horizons and will determine how far ahead they can really forecast. The advantage of analyzing the predictions made by a large number of professional forecasters is that abrupt structural and policy changes that are hard to pick up by estimated forecasting models can possibly be incorporated into the subjective judgments of experts. There seems to be a widely held expectation that the economy can be forecast over a typical business cycle, which is about five to seven years long. I will contrast two types of forecasts: 1) the actual growth rate and 2) whether the growth will be negative in some specified quarter in the future. I find that forecasts for the actual GDP growth do not have much value when the horizon goes beyond 18 months. However, the probability forecasts for negative GDP growth have no value when the horizon exceeds six months. I explore reasons why the directional probability forecasts perform worse than the quantitative real GDP forecasts.

INFORMATION CONTENT OF REAL GDP FORECASTS

In this section I analyze the quantitative forecasts using 15 years of monthly private-sector forecast data for 18 developed countries, reported over 24 different forecast horizons. The real GDP forecasts come from Consensus Economics Inc., an international economic survey organization. Since October 1989, Consensus Economics Inc. has been polling more than 600 forecasters each month and recording their forecasts for principal macroeconomic variables (including GDP growth, inflation, interest rates, and exchange rates) for a large number of countries. Forecasts are made for the current year (based on partial information about developments in that year) and for the following year. The number of forecasters ranges from 10 to 30 for most of the countries, and for the major industrialized countries the panelists are based in the countries for which they forecast.

We study the consensus forecasts of average annual real GDP growth. Survey respondents make their first forecasts when there are 24 months to the end of the year being forecast; that is, they start forecasting GDP growth in January of the previous year, and their last monthly forecast is reported at the beginning of December of the target year, 23 months later. So for each country and for each target year I have 24 forecasts of varying horizons. Our data set ranges from October 1989 to June 2004. The countries we study are the 18 industrialized countries for which forecasts are available from Consensus Economics Inc.[1]

In order to evaluate the forecast errors correctly, the forecasts should be matched with the actual data being forecast. It is well documented in the literature that data revisions may have an important impact on the perceived performance of the forecasters. Since forecasters cannot possibly be aware of data revisions after they report their forecasts, we use an early revision as the actual value, which is compiled from the midyear reports of the issue of *OECD Economic Outlook* immediately following the target year. However, because of the changes in variable definitions (i.e., GNP to GDP, or West Germany to unified Germany), some of the data are not available in the June issue of *OECD Economic Outlook*. We collected these data from the original sources, such as the May and June issues of the Bureau of Economic Analysis's *Survey of Business*, or issues of Deutsche Bundesbank's *Monthly Report* in the year immediately following the target year.

The information value of a forecast is related to how accurate the forecast is. In this section, we will provide statistics such as mean squared error (MSE), mean absolute error (MAE), and Theil's U-statistic, along with another statistic recently proposed by Diebold and Kilian (2001). Whereas MSE and MAE depend on the variability of the actual process, Theil's U-statistic scales the root mean square error (RMSE) by the variability of underlying data and has the advantage of being independent of the variance of the actual process. Formally,

$$(3.1) \quad U_h(y_n) = \sqrt{\frac{\sum_{t=1}^{T}(y_t - f_{t,h})^2}{\sum_{t=1}^{T}(y_t - y_n)^2}}.$$

Equation (3.1) compares the forecast errors with a naive forecast, y_n. If U_h is more than one, the forecast does not beat the naive forecast. An important issue in calculating the U_h is the selection of the naive forecast. In this study, we will follow the literature and use the forecast of no change as the naive forecast, i.e., $y_n = y_{t-1}$.

To see the improvement in the performance of forecasts over decreasing horizons, we also provide an R^2 measure, which is based on the idea of a predictability measure proposed by Diebold and Kilian (2001). They propose the measure of predictability as

$$p_{s,k} = 1 - \frac{E\left[L(e_s)\right]}{E\left[L(e_k)\right]},$$

where $E\left[L(e_k)\right]$ denotes the expected loss in the long-run forecasts and $E\left[L(e_s)\right]$ denotes the expected loss in the short-run forecasts. If MSE is used as the loss function, then we have

$$p_{s,k} = 1 - \frac{MSE_s}{MSE_k}.$$

Diebold and Kilian (2001) use this measure to compute the predictability of several macro variables using the realized data. Using k-period-ahead survey forecasts as the naive forecast, $p_{s,k}$ will give the improvement in the forecasts as horizon decreases.

Table 3.1 presents MAE, MSE, and Theil's U-statistics for 12- and 24-month-ahead forecasts. Later we also provide the Theil's U-statistics for all horizons. For 24-month-ahead forecasts, Theil's U-statistic is less than one for only Canada, Denmark, Germany, and the United States. The worst performers in 24-month-ahead forecasts are Portugal, Ireland, and the Netherlands, which have Theil's U-statistics of 1.45, 1.41, and 1.39, respectively. For 12-month-ahead forecasts, all the countries, with the exception of Ireland and Portugal, have Theil's U-statistics of less than one, implying that the forecasts have value over the no-change forecast.

Figure 3.1 presents Diebold and Kilian's $p_{h,24}$ and Theil's $U_h(y_{t-1})$ for each forecast horizon and country. Notice that large values of Theil's U imply large forecast errors. On the other hand, large values

Table 3.1 Goodness of Fit of Forecasts (MAE, RMSE, and Theil's U)

Country	12-month-ahead forecasts			24-month-ahead forecasts		
	MAE	RMSE	Theil's U	MAE	RMSE	Theil's U
Austria	0.98	1.16	0.81	1.24	1.48	1.01
Belgium	0.99	1.15	0.72	1.28	1.68	1.02
Canada	1.21	1.36	0.70	1.44	1.70	0.88
Denmark	0.72	0.99	0.75	0.96	1.14	0.84
Finland	2.24	2.89	0.87	2.70	3.37	1.07
France	0.79	0.99	0.73	1.15	1.50	1.08
Germany	0.79	1.03	0.60	1.49	1.96	0.99
Ireland	2.35	2.76	1.08	2.98	3.67	1.41
Italy	0.77	0.87	0.65	1.39	1.61	1.19
Japan	1.41	1.58	0.74	1.90	2.30	1.04
Netherlands	0.89	1.06	0.88	1.38	1.72	1.39
Norway	0.92	1.13	0.73	1.14	1.33	1.00
Portugal	0.98	1.31	1.02	1.40	1.89	1.45
Spain	0.61	0.86	0.66	1.18	1.58	1.20
Sweden	0.90	1.13	0.69	1.46	1.84	1.13
Switzerland	1.22	1.45	0.92	1.71	2.04	1.26
United Kingdom	0.77	1.02	0.70	1.08	1.62	1.12
United States	0.96	1.09	0.64	1.28	1.59	0.96

SOURCE: Author's own research.

of $p_{h,24}$ imply that forecasts improve significantly over the 24-month-ahead forecast $f_{t,24}$. The right axes in the figures show $p_{h,24}$, whereas the left axes show the values of $U_h(y_{t-1})$. Since 1.0 is the threshold value of $U_h(y_{t-1})$ for determining whether the forecast can beat the naive forecast of no change, the plots in Figure 3.1 include a horizontal line through 1.0. In addition, to pinpoint the longest horizon at which the forecasts beat the naive forecast, the graphs also include a vertical line through the longest horizon at which the estimated $U_h(y_{t-1})$ is lower than one. This provides an easy way to compare the countries with each other. For all the countries, as the forecast horizon decreases, the quality of the forecasts increases, as expected. The graphs also point out significant heterogeneity across countries.

When we look at the performance rankings based on Theil's $U_h(y_{t-1})$, we observe that in addition to the four country forecasts that

Figure 3.1 Information Content of Forecasts over Horizons, October 1989–June 2004

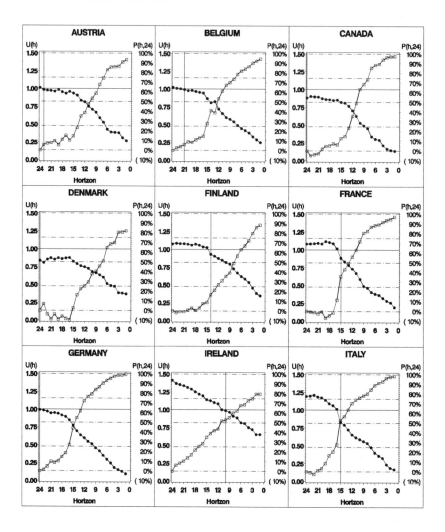

Figure 3.1 (continued)

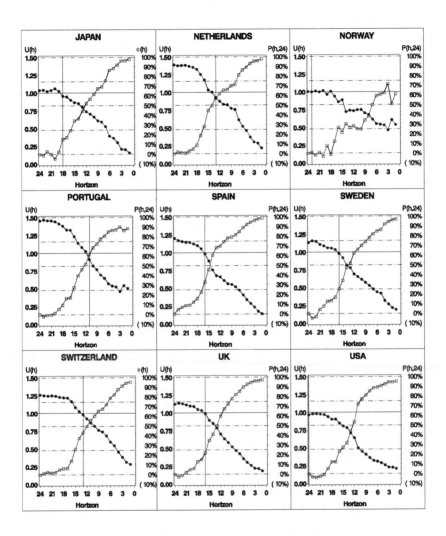

NOTE: $U(h)$ = Theil's U; $P(h,24)$ = Diebold-Kilian predictability statistic.
SOURCE: Author's analysis of data from the SPF.

beat the naive forecast when horizon is 24 months (i.e., the American, Danish, German, and Canadian forecasts given in Table 3.1), we now see that Austrian and Norwegian forecasts beat the naive forecast when the horizon is 23 months. In terms of the worst performances in beating the naive forecast, we find that the Irish and Portuguese forecasts beat the naive forecast at horizons of 10 and 11 months, respectively. These are followed by Switzerland and the Netherlands, which beat the naive forecast when the horizon is 13 months.

The Diebold-Kilian measure of predictability, $p_{h,24}$, shows the improvement in the information content of the forecasts as measured by the decrease in the mean squared errors over the MSE of the 24-month-ahead forecasts. As shown in Figure 3.1, the predictive ability of GDP forecasts for some countries (e.g., France, Canada, Denmark, Finland, Japan, and the United States) does not improve over the 24-month-ahead forecasts when the horizon is relatively long, but for some other countries (e.g., Germany, Ireland, and Spain), each additional month increases the information content of the forecasts over the previous month, even in longer-run forecasts. For most of the countries, we see that MSE substantially decreases in the short-run forecasts, causing $p_{h,24}$ to be close to 100 percent when the forecast horizon is one month. Two exceptions are the Norwegian and Irish GDP growth forecasts, where the final values of $p_{h,24}$ are less than 80 percent.

EXPLORING THE DATA-GENERATING PROCESSES

We find that, historically, real GDP has been a difficult variable to predict beyond 24 months at the maximum. One might think that this can be attributed to the variability of the underlying series. However, it is not the variability but rather the predictability of the target variable that is one of the important factors in the analysis. This is the focus of this section.

Following Galbraith (2003) and Galbraith and Tkacz (2007), we calculate the forecast content and content horizons for the quarterly GDP growth rate for all seven countries in our sample over the period 1990–2007. The forecast content is defined as the proportionate gain in the MSE from the best-fitting autoregressive model over the unconditional mean of the series as the benchmark. The forecast content horizon is defined as the horizon beyond which the forecast content is close to zero. Galbraith (2003) has characterized the content function of AR(p) models analytically, taking into account the uncertainty associated with parameter estimation. We allow p to be no greater than 4 for quarterly GDP data. The value of p is chosen by the Schwarz information criterion, using an upper bound. The benchmark values were the unconditional means of the individual series during 1990–2007. All the data used in this section are downloaded from Datastream, a financial statistical database from Thomson Reuters.

The results of the estimation of forecast content functions for seven industrialized countries are presented in Figure 3.2. For annual GDP growth using quarterly data, the forecast content becomes less than 0.05 when the horizon exceeds six quarters. These findings are consistent

Figure 3.2 Real GDP Predictability Based on AR(p) Models (quarterly horizons)

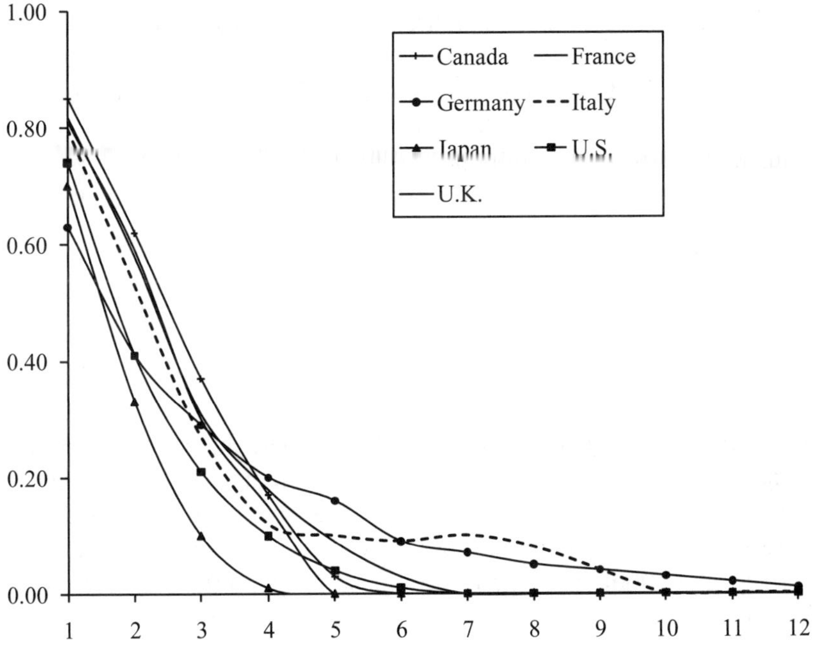

SOURCE: Author's analysis of SPF data.

with the results reported in Galbraith (2003), who has looked at the predictability of GDP and inflation for Canada and the United States.

We should point out that our forecast content functions are based purely on linear autoregressive models of the target variables. In reality, forecast content and predictability can be and possibly are improved upon by incorporating additional information and using more complicated models.[2] In addition, the forecast content functions are typically estimated using currently available revised data. For variables like real GDP that go through a substantial amount of data revision, their predictability in real time can be quite different. Since the variance of the early revisions of a variable is necessarily less than that of the revised series, the predictability of a series may seem to be less attractive than what one may get using real-time data. In that sense, the forecast content from the simple AR model provides an overall *lower* bound on the true predictability of a series. For real GDP, Croushore (2006) reports mixed evidence as to the effect of data revisions on predictability, depending on the sample period. Since data revisions are relatively small for inflation, they have very little effect on predictability. In our analysis, the relative ranking of different countries in terms of RMSE does not match the relative ranking of those countries in terms of forecast content horizons that one obtains from Galbraith's method for the variable. The ranking can also depend on the specific benchmark used in the analysis. Thus it is necessary to study the predictability of real GDP by professional forecasters in real time with respect to a more natural benchmark.

EVALUATING PROBABILITY FORECASTS FOR REAL GDP DECLINES

In this section I report on the value of the subjective probability forecasts that are obtained from the SPF as predictors of GDP downturns. Even though these forecasts have been available since 1968 and have drawn media attention, very little systematic analysis has been conducted to look into their usefulness as possible business cycle indicators.[3]

One purpose of this section is to illustrate that an evaluation of recorded probability forecasts by professional economists can suggest reasons for forecasting failures and can help define limits to the current capability of macroeconomic forecasts. The traditional and the most popular way of evaluating probability forecasts is the MSE type of measure, such as Brier's quadratic probability score (QPS), which evaluates the external correspondence between the probability forecasts and the realization of the event. This approach, however, can fail to identify the ability of a forecasting system to evaluate the odds of the occurrence of an event against its nonoccurrence, which is a very important characteristic to the users of forecasts. A high performance score can be achieved by totally unskilled forecasts having little information value. Thus, the traditional approach can be inadequate in evaluating the usefulness of probability forecasts, particularly for rare events.[4]

The SPF has been collecting subjective probability forecasts of real GDP/GNP declines during the current and four subsequent quarters since its inception in 1968.[5] At the end of the first month of each quarter, the individual forecasters in the SPF form their forecasts. The survey collects probability assessments for a decline in real GDP in the current quarter and in each of the next four quarters, conditional on the growth in the current period. The number of respondents has varied between 15 and 60 over the quarters. Since our aim in this study is to evaluate the SPF probability forecasts at the macro level, we use forecasts averaged over individuals. Using the July revisions, during our sample period from the fourth quarter of 1968 to the second quarter of 2004, there were 20 quarters of negative GDP growth spread out over six periods, variously beginning in 1969:4, 1973:4, 1980:1, 1981:3, 1990:3, and 2001:1. These made up six separate episodes of real GDP declines. Thus, only about 14 percent of quarters in the entire sample of 143 quarters exhibited negative GDP growth. The annualized real-time real GDP growth issued every July is used as the forecasting target, against which the forecasting performance of the SPF forecasts will be evaluated.

As noted above, the traditional way of evaluating probability forecasts for the occurrence of a binary event is to assess the calibration of the forecasts against realizations—that is, to assess the external correspondence between the probability forecasts and the actual occurrence of the event. A measure-oriented approach simply compares the forecast probabilities with the realization of a binary event, which is represented by a dummy variable taking value 1 or 0, depending upon the occurrence of the event. The most commonly used measure is Brier's QPS, a probability analog of mean squared error. Thus,

$$(3.2) \quad QPS = 1/T \sum_{t=1}^{T} (f_t - x_t)^2 ,$$

where f_t is the forecast probability made at time t, x_t is the realization of the event (1 if the event occurs and 0 otherwise) at time t, and T is the total number of the observations—or forecasting quarters in our case.

The QPS ranges from 0 to 1, with a score of 0 corresponding to perfect accuracy, and is a function only of the difference between the assessed probabilities and realizations. The calculated quadratic probability scores for each forecasting horizon from the current quarter (Q0) to the next four quarters (Q1, Q2, Q3, and Q4) are calculated to be 0.077, 0.098, 0.103, 0.124, and 0.127, respectively. Thus, even though these scores deteriorate as the forecast horizon increases, all seem to suggest good calibration and are close to zero.

RECEIVER (OR RELATIVE) OPERATING CHARACTERISTIC (ROC)

In evaluating rare event probabilities, it is crucial to minimize the impact of the predominant outcome on the outcome score. More specifically, the impact of correctly identifying the frequent event, which is the primary source of the hedging, should be minimized. So a better approach to forecast performance should concentrate on the hit rate and false alarm rate of the infrequent event, instead of the "percentage correctly predicted" that is the very basis of QPS (Doswell, Davies-Jones, and Keller 1990; Murphy 1991).

A simple and often-used measure of forecast skill, the Kuipers score, or KS—sometimes referred to as the Pierce skill score—is obtained by taking the difference between the hit rate (H) and the false alarm rate (F), where H is the proportion of the number of times an event was forecast to the number of times it occurred, and F is the proportion of the number of times the event was forecast to the number of times it did not occur. Given a decision threshold w, the contingency table for successes and failures for the event can be written as in Table 3.2. Then the

Table 3.2 Schematic Contingency Table

Event forecast	Event occurred	Event did not occur	Total
Yes	a (hit)	b (false alarm)	$a + b$
No	c (miss)	d (correct rejection)	$c + d$
Total	$a + c$	$b + d$	$a + b + c + d = T$

NOTE: T = total number of observations.
SOURCE: Author's own research.

KS can be calculated as $H - F = (ad - bc) / ([a + c] [b + d])$. Assuming independence of the hit and false alarm rates, the asymptotic standard error of the KS is given by

$$\sqrt{[H(1 - H) / (a + c)] + [F(1 - F) / (b + d)]} \ .$$

(See Agresti [1996].) Alternatively, based on the market-timing test of Pesaran and Timmermann (1992), Granger and Pesaran (2000a,b) have suggested an alternative test for the significance of the Kuipers test,

$$PT = \sqrt{T} KS / \sqrt{P_x(1 - P_x) / x(1 - x)}, \text{ where } P_x = x H + (1 - x)F.$$

Stephenson (2000) notes that if one of the two elements in a column of the contingency table (e.g., d) is very large, then the Kuipers skill score effectively disregards the other element (e.g., b) almost completely. This can be a limitation of the KS in evaluating rare event forecasts.

Instead, the forecast skill can better be judged by comparing the odds of making a good forecast (a hit) to the odds of making a bad forecast (a false alarm)—i.e., by using the odds ratio $\theta = [H/(1 - H)]/[F/(1 - F)]$, which is simply equal to the cross-product ratio $(ad)/(bc)$ obtainable from the contingency table. The odds ratio is unity when the forecasts and the realizations are independent or $KS = 0$, and can be easily tested for significance by considering the log odds, which are approximately normal with a standard error, given by

$$\sqrt{1/a + 1/b + 1/c + 1/d} \ .$$

Note that each cell count should be at least 5 for the validity of the approximation. *KS* and *θ* are reported in Table 3.3 for relevant values of the decision threshold *w*.

One important but often overlooked issue in the evaluation of probability forecasts is the role of the selected threshold. The performance of a probability forecast in terms of discrimination ability is actually the result of the combination of the intrinsic discrimination ability of a forecasting system and the selection of the threshold. In this regard, the receiver (or relative) operating characteristic (ROC) is a convenient descriptive approach, but unfortunately has drawn little attention in econometrics.[6]

The decision to issue a forecast for occurrence or nonoccurrence of an event is typically made based on a predetermined threshold (say, *w*) on the weight of evidence scale *W*. The occurrence forecast is announced if $W > w$; the nonoccurrence is announced otherwise. ROC can be represented by a graph of the hit rate against the false alarm rate as *w* varies, with the false alarm rate plotted as the *x* axis and the hit rate as the *y* axis. The location of the entire curve in the unit square is determined by the intrinsic discrimination capacity of the forecasts, and the location of specific points on a curve is determined by the decision threshold *w* that is selected by the user. As the decision threshold *w* varies from low to high, or the ROC curve moves from right to left, *H* and *F* vary together to trace out the ROC curve. Low thresholds lead to both high *H* and high *F*, found toward the upper-right-hand corner. Conversely, high thresholds make the ROC points move toward the lower-left-hand corner along the curve. Thus, a perfect discrimination is represented by an ROC that rises from (0,0) along the *y* axis to (0,1), then straight right to (1,1). The diagonal $H = F$ represents zero skill, indicating that the forecasts are completely nondiscriminatory. ROC points below the diagonal represent the same level of skill as they would if they were located above the diagonal and are merely mislabeled—i.e., a forecast of nonoccurrence should be taken as occurrence.

Figures 3.3A–3.3E display the ROC curves, together with their 95 percent confidence intervals for the current quarter and the next four quarters. The confidence interval was calculated using the formula

$$\frac{\hat{H} + \dfrac{z_{\alpha/2}^2}{2T} \pm z_{\alpha/2}\left\{[\hat{H}(1-\hat{H}) + \dfrac{z_{\alpha/2}^2}{4T}]/T\right\}^{1/2}}{1 + z_{\alpha/2}^2/T}$$

for each w, where $z_{a/2} = z_{0.025} = 1.96$ for a standard normal variate. It can be seen that the ROC for the current quarter (Q0) is located maximally away from the diagonal towards the left upper corner, demonstrating the highest discrimination ability of the SPF forecasts, followed by the one-quarter-ahead forecasts. For longer-term forecasts, ROCs become rapidly flatter as the forecasting horizon increases. For the four-quarter-ahead (Q4) forecasts, the ROC mildly snakes around the diagonal line, and the associated confidence band suggests that practically none of the values are statistically different from the values on the diagonal line. This means that the Q4 forecasts have no skill or discrimination ability for any value of the threshold. In situations where the analyst may have only a vague idea about the relative costs of type I and type II errors (e.g., in the problem of predicting the turning point in a business cycle), he or she can pick a comfortable hit rate (or false alarm rate) of choice, and the underlying ROC curve will give the corresponding false alarm rate (or hit rate). This will also give an optimal threshold for making decisions. When the relative costs of the two types of errors are known exactly, the decision-theoretic framework developed by Zellner, Hong, and Min (1991) and Granger and Pesaran (2000a,b) can be used to issue recession signals. However, before using the probability forecasts in decision making, the significance of their skillfulness should first be established.

The hit rates and false alarm rates for selected threshold values in the range 0.50–0.05 are reported in Table 3.3, where one can find the mix of hit and false alarm rates that is expected to be associated with each horizon-specific forecast.[7] For example, for achieving a hit rate of 90 percent with Q0 forecasts, one should use 0.25 as the threshold, and the corresponding false alarm rate is expected to be 0.16. Table 3.3 also shows that at this threshold value, even though the false alarm rates are roughly around 0.15 for forecasts of all horizons, the hit rate steadily declines, from 90 percent for Q0 to only 21 percent for Q4. This clearly documents the rapid speed of deterioration in forecast capability as the forecast horizon increases. Though not reported in Table 3.3, for the same hit rate of 90 percent, the false alarm rates for Q1–Q4 forecasts are 0.189 ($w = 0.237$), 0.636 ($w = 0.13$), 0.808 ($w = 0.115$), and 0.914 ($w = 0.10$), respectively. Thus, for the same hit rate, the corresponding false alarm rates for Q3–Q4 forecasts are so large (80 percent and 91 percent, respectively) that they can be considered useless for all practical purposes, and thus may have very little value in decision making.

Figure 3.3 Trade-Off between Hit Rates and False Alarm Rates at Different Horizons

Panel A: ROC for Q0 ± 95 Percent Band

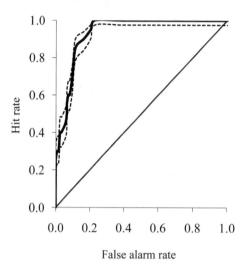

Panel B: ROC for Q1 ± 95 Percent Band

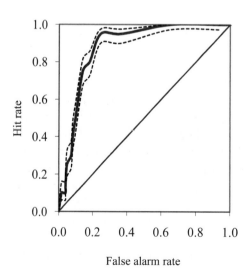

Figure 3.3 (continued)

Panel C: ROC for Q2 ± 95 Percent Band

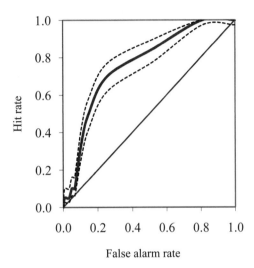

Panel D: ROC for Q3 ± 95 Percent Band

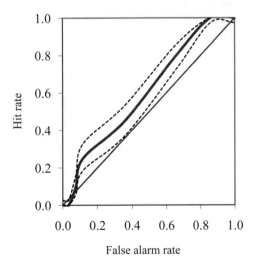

Figure 3.3 (continued)

Panel E: ROC for Q4 ± 95 Percent Band

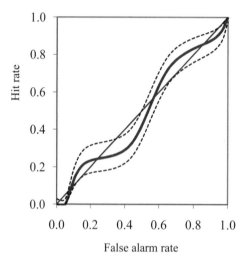

NOTE: ROC = receiver (or relative) operating characteristic.
SOURCE: Author's analysis of SPF data.

In Table 3.3 we have also reported the Kuipers scores (KS) and the odds ratios (θ) for selected w. The rapid decline in these values as the forecast horizon increases is remarkable, and for Q4 forecasts these values are close to zero and unity, respectively, suggesting no skill. Using the critical value 1.645 for a one-sided normal test at the 5 percent level, the KS and θ values were found to be statistically significant for Q0–Q2 and insignificant for Q4 forecasts.[8] For Q3 forecasts, there is some conflicting evidence, depending on the tests we use. Based on the standard error formula

$$\sqrt{[H(1-H)/(a+c)]+[F(1-F)/(b+d)]}$$

for KS reported in Agresti (1996), KS values for Q3 were insignificant at the 5 percent level for all allowable values of w. However, the Pesaran-Timmermann (PT) test and the test based on the log odds ratio for Q3 were statistically significant only for $w = 0.25$, even at the 1 percent level. Notwithstanding this result, the weight of our previous evidence suggests that Q3 forecasts have very little skill. We should, however, emphasize that statistical significance or insignificance does not mean the forecasts have utility or value in a particular decision-theoretic context.[9]

I find overwhelming evidence that Q0–Q2 forecasts have good operating characteristics. Given the relative costs of two types of classification errors, the end user can choose an appropriate threshold w to minimize the total expected cost of misclassification. This type of optimal decision rule cannot be obtained by only studying QPS. More importantly, for forecasting relatively rare events like recessions, ROC and odds ratios are useful for making sure that the probability forecasts have operational value. This is because, in this approach, the success rate in predicting the predominant event is not part of the goodness of fit measure.

CONCLUDING REMARKS

In this chapter I first report the characteristics of fixed-target monthly GDP growth forecasts for 18 developed countries during the period 1989–2004. I show how forecasting performance improves as the forecast horizon decreases, and at what horizons forecasts start to become informative. Since there are many forecasting organizations around the world that provide forecasts for many macroeconomic variables, with horizons of up to 12 quarters or more, it is interesting to explore the value of these forecasts and thereby try to understand the limits to how far ahead today's professional forecasters can reasonably predict these variables. Since the panel of forecasters in Consensus Economics Inc. are all private-market professionals, the limits to forecasting that these professionals exhibit can safely be taken as indicative of the current state of economic forecasting. I find wide diversity in the quality of the forecasts across countries, and in the horizons at which forecasts start becoming useful—possibly reflecting the forecast difficulty of the underlying series.

Table 3.3 Measures of Forecast Skill: Quarter 0 to Quarter 4

w	Q0				Q1				Q2				Q3				Q4			
	H	F	Kuipers score	Odds ratio	H	F	Kuipers score	Odds ratio	H	F	Kuipers score	Odds ratio	H	F	Kuipers score	Odds ratio	H	F	Kuipers score	Odds ratio
0.50	0.55	0.07	0.48	17.57	0.25	0.05	0.20	6.44	0.05	0.03	0.02	1.54	0.00	0.00	0.00	—	0.00	0.00	0.00	—
0.45	0.60	0.07	0.53	19.00	0.30	0.07	0.23	5.38	0.10	0.05	0.05	2.13	0.00	0.00	0.00	—	0.00	0.00	0.00	—
0.40	0.60	0.08	0.52	16.95	0.40	0.08	0.32	7.47	0.10	0.07	0.03	1.57	0.00	0.00	0.00	—	0.00	0.00	0.00	—
0.35	0.70	0.10	0.60	21.58	0.50	0.10	0.40	9.17	0.15	0.07	0.08	2.20	0.00	0.03	−0.03	0.00	0.00	0.00	0.00	—
0.30	0.85	0.11	0.74	44.12	0.75	0.14	0.61	18.53	0.35	0.11	0.24	4.47	0.10	0.08	0.03	1.37	0.00	0.05	−0.05	0.00
0.25	0.90	0.16	0.74	46.35	0.80	0.18	0.62	18.18	0.50	0.15	0.35	5.72	0.25	0.12	0.13	2.52	0.21	0.16	0.06	1.45
0.20	0.95	0.20	0.75	74.48	0.95	0.25	0.70	58.27	0.70	0.26	0.44	6.77	0.45	0.36	0.09	1.47	0.32	0.43	−0.12	0.61
0.15	1.00	0.23	0.77	—	0.95	0.37	0.58	32.51	0.85	0.53	0.32	5.05	0.80	0.66	0.14	2.08	0.74	0.66	0.07	1.42
0.10	1.00	0.40	0.60	—	1.00	0.66	0.34	—	1.00	0.81	0.19	—	1.00	0.86	0.14	—	0.89	0.93	−0.04	0.63
0.05	1.00	0.68	0.32	—	1.00	0.94	0.06	—	1.00	0.99	0.01	—	1.00	1.00	0.00	—	1.00	1.00	0.00	—

NOTE: w = decision threshold; H = hit rate; F = false alarm rate; — = not defined.
SOURCE: Author's own research.

I use Theil's U-statistic with the lagged GDP growth as the benchmark, as well as another measure of predictability recently suggested by Diebold and Kilian (2001) with the two-year-ahead forecast as the benchmark. In terms of Theil's U, for only 7 of the 18 countries (Austria, Belgium, Canada, Denmark, Germany, Norway, and the United States) did the initial 24-month-ahead forecasts beat the naive forecast. In terms of the worst performance, the Irish, Portuguese, Swiss, and Dutch forecasts beat the naive forecast at horizons as late as 10–13 months.

In terms of the Diebold-Kilian skill measure, I find that for the majority of the countries, the long-term forecasts for up to 18 months are as good as the initial 24-month-ahead forecasts. That is, over these longer horizons, forecasters do not receive dependable information with which to adjust their forecasts systematically. I also observe a similar pattern when I look at the horizons at which the survey forecasts beat the naive no-change forecast. These findings imply that the survey forecasts do not have much value when the horizon goes beyond 18 months or so.

I then go on to evaluate the subjective probability forecasts for real GDP declines during the period 1968–2004, using methodologies developed in psychology and meteorology. The SPF records probability forecasts for real GDP declines during the current and next four quarters. I find overwhelming evidence that the shorter-run forecasts (Q0–Q2) possess significant skill. In contrast, Q3 and Q4 forecasts exhibit poor performance, as measured by ROC measures. It is clear from my analysis that our professional forecasters do not have adequate information to forecast GDP declines meaningfully at horizons beyond two quarters; they lack relevant discriminatory cues. Since the SPF panel is composed of professional economists and business analysts who forecast on the basis of models and informed heuristics, their failure in the long-term forecasts may indicate that, at the present time, forecasting real GDP growth beyond two quarters may not be possible with reasonable type I and type II errors. Since survey probabilities embody important additional information over point forecasts, an analysis of the probability forecasts provides us with a unique opportunity to understand the reasons for forecast failures. Our analysis of probability forecasts suggests that it is more challenging to predict a GDP decline or a recession than quantitative growth rate. This is because in predicting a relatively uncommon event like real GDP decline, the time series property and the persistence of the series are less useful than forecasting the quantitative GDP growth rate.

I have emphasized that for forecasting rare events like recessions, it is important to examine the ROC curves, where the relative odds for the event can be studied in depth. The analysis also helps find an optimum probability threshold for transforming the probability forecasts to a binary decision rule. In many instances the selection of the threshold is quite arbitrary. In this regard, ROC analysis provides a simple but an objective criterion, incorporating the end user's loss function for missed signals and false alarms. The ROC analysis in our case reveals that for a preassigned hit rate of, say, 90 percent, the associated false alarm rates for the Q3–Q4 forecasts are so high that they may be considered useless for all practical purposes.

One wonders if the professional forecasters can be trained to do better. In the current situation, forecasting improvement may not be possible for various reasons. In most psychological and Bayesian learning experiments, the outcomes are readily available and are known with certainty; thus, prompt feedback for the purpose of improvement is possible. In contrast, the GDP figures are announced with considerable lag time, and are then revised repeatedly. Also, as I have mentioned before, correct and dependable cues for predicting recessions a few quarters ahead may not be available to economists. The excess variability of forecasts and the observed lack of discriminating ability may just be a reflection of that hard reality. It may be the same reason that model-based forecasts over business-cycle frequencies have not succeeded in the past.

Finally, I should point out that the relative inferiority of real GDP forecasts can also be determined by the demand side of the forecasting market—i.e., the professional forecasters may devote more efforts to generating better forecasts if their clients demand that. It is interesting that as part of the Fed's major changes in its communication strategies, which took effect in September 2007, the horizon of the projections for GDP growth and inflation by all FOMC members has been extended from two years to three.[10] As I report earlier in this chapter, currently the real GDP growth forecasts do not seem to have any value beyond the 18-month horizon. If the demand side of the forecasting market has any effect on forecast quality, we may expect that, as a result of this change in FOMC policy, the content horizon for these forecasts will lengthen in the future.

Notes

1. See Isiklar and Lahiri (2007) and Isiklar, Lahiri, and Loungani (2006) for further details on the data.
2. Galbraith and Tkacz (2007) have, however, found that forecast horizons do not improve even when dynamic factor models with many predictors are used in place of simple univariate autoregressive models.
3. Notable exceptions include Braun and Yaniv (1992), Graham (1996), Lahiri and Wang (2006), and Stock and Watson (2003). However, these studies emphasized different aspects of the data. More recently, Clements (2009) has studied the relationship between intrapersonal uncertainty and interpersonal disagreement in these forecasts. Details of this data set are described in Lahiri and Wang (2008).
4. See Doswell, Davies-Jones, and Keller (1990), Lahiri and Wang (2006), Murphy (1991), and Stephenson (2000) for more discussion on this issue.
5. See Croushore (1993) for an introduction to the SPF.
6. This approach has a long history in medical imaging, and has also been used in evaluating loan default and rating forecasts (Hanley and McNeil 1982; Stein 2005). See Jolliffe and Stephenson (2003), Stephenson (2000), and Swets and Pickett (1982) for additional analysis of the use of ROC.
7. In order to save space, we did not report in Table 3.3 the values of w greater than 0.5. Moreover, these values were less relevant in our context.
8. Note that the cell counts were in excess of 5 only in cases of w values (0.50–0.35) for Q0, (0.45–0.35) for Q1, (0.30–0.20) for Q2, (0.25–0.20) for Q3, and (0.20–0.15) for Q4. The significance tests were conducted only for these cases.
9. Granger and Pesaran (2000a) show how, under certain simplifying assumptions, the Kuipers score can be used as an indicator of economic value.
10. See Bernanke (2007).

References

Agresti, Alan. 1996. *An Introduction to Categorical Data Analysis.* New York: John Wiley and Sons.

Bernanke, Ben. 2007. "Federal Reserve Communications." Speech delivered at the Cato Institute's 25th Annual Monetary Conference, "Monetary Arrangements in the 21st Century," held in Washington, DC, November 14.

Braun, Phillip A., and Ilan Yaniv. 1992. "A Case Study of Expert Judgment: Economists' Probabilities versus Base-Rate Model Forecasts." *Journal of Behavioral Decision Making* 5(3): 217–231.

Clements, Michael P. 2009. "Internal Consistency of Survey Respondents' Forecasts: Evidence Based on the Survey of Professional Forecasters." In *The Methodology and Practice of Econometrics: A Festschrift in Honour of David F. Hendry*, Jennifer L. Castle and Neil Shephard, eds. Oxford: Oxford University Press, pp. 206–226.

Croushore, Dean. 1993. "Introducing: The Survey of Professional Forecasters." Federal Reserve Bank of Philadelphia *Business Review* 1993(November/December): 3–15.

————. 2006. "Forecasting with Real-Time Macroeconomic Data." In *Handbook of Economic Forecasting*, Vol. 1, Graham Elliott, Clive W.J. Granger, and Allan Timmermann, eds. Amsterdam: North-Holland, pp. 961–982.

Diebold, Francis X., and Lutz Kilian. 2001. "Measuring Predictability: Theory and Macroeconomic Applications." *Journal of Applied Econometrics* 16(6): 657–669.

Doswell, Charles A. III, Robert Davies-Jones, and David L. Keller. 1990. "On Summary Measures of Skill in Rare Event Forecasting Based on Contingency Tables." *Weather and Forecasting* 5(4): 576–585.

Galbraith, John W. 2003. "Content Horizons for Univariate Time-Series Forecasts." *International Journal of Forecasting* 19(1): 43–55.

Galbraith, John W., and Greg Tkacz. 2007. "Forecast Content and Content Horizons for Some Important Macroeconomic Time Series." *Canadian Journal of Economics* 40(3): 935–953.

Graham, John R. 1996. "Is a Group of Economists Better Than One? Than None?" *Journal of Business* 69(2): 193–232.

Granger, Clive W.J. 1996. "Can We Improve the Perceived Quality of Economic Forecasts?" *Journal of Applied Econometrics* 11(5): 455–473.

Granger, Clive W.J., and M. Hashem Pesaran. 2000a. "A Decision Theoretic Approach to Forecast Evaluation." In *Statistics and Finance: An Interface*, Wai-Sum Chen, Wai Keung Li, and Howell Tong, eds. London: Imperial College Press, pp. 261–276.

————. 2000b. "Economic and Statistical Measures of Forecast Accuracy." *Journal of Forecasting* 19(7): 537–560.

Hanley, James A., and Barbara J. McNeil. 1982. "The Meaning and Use of the Area under a Receiver Operating Characteristic (ROC) Curve." *Radiology* 143(1): 29–36.

Isiklar, Gultekin, and Kajal Lahiri. 2007. "How Far Ahead Can We Forecast? Evidence from Cross-Country Surveys." *International Journal of Forecasting* 23(2): 167–187.

Isiklar, Gultekin, Kajal Lahiri, and Prakash Loungani. 2006. " How Quickly Do Forecasters Incorporate News? Evidence from Cross-Country Surveys." *Journal of Applied Econometrics* 21(6): 703–725.

Jolliffe, Ian T., and David B. Stephenson, eds. 2003. *Forecast Verification: A Practitioner's Guide in Atmospheric Science*. Chichester, W. Sussex, UK: John Wiley and Sons.

Lahiri, Kajal, and J. George Wang. 2006. "Subjective Probability Forecasts for Recessions: Evaluations and Guidelines for Use." *Business Economics* 41(2): 26–37.

———. 2008. "Evaluating Probability Forecasts for GDP Declines." Discussion paper. Albany, NY: University at Albany, State University of New York.

Makridakis, Spyros, Robin M. Hogarth, and Anil Gaba. 2009. "Forecasting and Uncertainty in the Economics and Business World." *International Journal of Forecasting* 25(4): 794–812.

Murphy, Allan H. 1991. "Forecaster's Forum: Probabilities, Odds, and Forecasters of Rare Events." *Weather and Forecasting* 6(2): 302–307.

Pesaran, M. Hashem, and Allan Timmermann. 1992. "A Simple Nonparametric Test of Predictive Performance." *Journal of Business and Economic Statistics* 10(4): 461–465.

Stein, Roger M. 2005. "The Relationship between Default Prediction and Lending Profits: Integrating ROC Analysis and Loan Pricing." *Journal of Banking and Finance* 29(5): 1213–1236.

Stephenson, David B. 2000. "Use of the 'Odds Ratio' for Diagnosing Forecast Skill." *Weather and Forecasting* 15(2): 221–232.

Stock, James H., and Mark W. Watson. 2003. "How Did Leading Indicator Forecasts Perform during the 2001 Recession?" Federal Reserve Bank of Richmond *Economic Quarterly* 89(3): 71–90.

Swets, John A., and Ronald M. Pickett. 1982. *Evaluation of Diagnostic Systems. Methods from Signal Detection Theory*. New York: Academic Press.

Zellner, Arnold, Chansik Hong, and Chung-ki Min. 1991. "Forecasting Turning Points in International Output Growth Rates Using Bayesian Exponentially Weighted Autoregression, Time-Varying Parameter, and Pooling Techniques." *Journal of Econometrics* 49(1–2): 275–304.

4

Forecasting Regional and Industry-Level Variables

Challenges and Strategies

David E. Rapach
Saint Louis University

Forecasting regional and industry-level (RIL) variables is an important task for a wide variety of economic agents. Policymakers at all levels of government utilize such forecasts, including local and state governments when planning budgets and the Federal Reserve when formulating U.S. monetary policy (e.g., the *Beige Book*). Businesses in the private sector also rely on such forecasts as inputs when taking employment, production, and investment decisions. The recent "Great Recession" highlights the relevance of forecasting RIL variables for policymakers and businesses: revenue reductions make accurate forecasts imperative for planning purposes and the efficient allocation of now-more-limited resources.

Forecasting almost any economic variable is, of course, extremely challenging. Nevertheless, forecasting RIL variables exacerbates typical forecasting difficulties. In particular, there are usually a plethora of potential predictors—global, national, regional, and industry variables—that are relevant for forecasting RIL variables. While theoretical models help to identify key determinants of a given RIL variable, such models are usually highly stylized and thus do not necessarily provide the most appropriate forecasting specifications, especially given the various idiosyncrasies surrounding individual RIL variables. A forecaster thus faces substantial *model uncertainty*. While the forecaster could include all potential predictors in a single forecasting model, such highly parameterized models usually fare very poorly in terms of out-of-sample forecasting, due in no small part to model uncertainty.[1]

Alternatively, the forecaster could preselect a relatively small number of predictors, but this ignores the potentially useful information available in the excluded variables. In this chapter, I outline some tractable approaches for incorporating information from a large number of potential predictors that avoid overly parameterized specifications. Recent research indicates that such approaches are quite beneficial for improving forecasts of RIL variables.

In addition to model uncertainty, *model instability* is a serious concern for forecasting RIL variables. Changes in institutions, public policy, and technology, among many other factors, can precipitate structural breaks that cause the predictive power of individual variables to vary significantly over time. Moreover, it is extremely difficult to predict the occurrence of structural breaks. Similar to model uncertainty, model instability causes highly parameterized models to break down in out-of-sample forecasting, so that a forecaster of RIL variables needs tractable approaches that are reasonably robust to structural breaks. Fortunately, approaches useful for dealing with model uncertainty also appear helpful for mitigating structural instability when forecasting RIL variables.

I outline three approaches—1) general-to-specific modeling with bagging (GETS-bagging), 2) forecast combination, and 3) factor models—for improving forecasts of RIL variables. GETS-bagging and forecast combination are methods for utilizing, in a tractable manner, information from a large set of potential predictors that are reasonably robust to model uncertainty and instability. Factor models focus on potentially strong relationships between RIL and national variables. I provide intuition and guidance on implementing these approaches. In addition, I discuss empirical results from recent research on forecasting RIL variables, highlighting examples pertaining to forecasting employment growth for Michigan and Missouri.

It is important to stress that the present chapter is relatively brief and is not meant as an exhaustive literature survey. Instead, it is intended to introduce the reader to strategies for improving forecasts of RIL variables from the recent literature—strategies designed to address the keen challenges posed by model uncertainty and instability.[2]

FORECASTING STRATEGIES

This section outlines forecasting approaches aimed at improving forecasts of RIL variables. I begin with a general ("kitchen sink") model that serves to illustrate some of the pitfalls that the GETS-bagging, combination, and factor model approaches are designed to avoid.

Kitchen-Sink Model

Consider the following general model specification:

$$(4.1) \quad \Delta y_{k,t+h}^{h} = a_k + b_k \Delta y_{k,t} + \sum_{i=1}^{N} c_{k,i} x_{i,t} + e_{k,t+h}^{h} ,$$

where t denotes the time period, $\Delta y_{k,t+h}^{h} = (1/h) \sum_{j=1}^{h} \Delta y_{k,t+j}$, $\Delta y_{k,t} = y_{k,t} - y_{k,t-1}$, $y_{k,t}$ is in log-levels, and $e_{k,t+h}^{h}$ is a zero-mean disturbance term. The left-hand side of Equation (4.1) is a cumulative growth rate for the variable of interest that we wish to forecast.[3] The k subscript indicates that $y_{k,t}$ is an RIL variable, where k indexes the region or industry. The $x_{i,t}$ variables $(i = 1, \ldots, N)$ on the right-hand side of Equation (4.1) represent N potential predictors of $\Delta y_{k,t+h}^{h}$, where N can be large. For expositional and notational simplicity, the right-hand side of Equation (4.1) includes only a single lag of $\Delta y_{k,t}$ and each $x_{i,t}$ variable; it is straightforward to allow for additional lags and thus a more general dynamic structure.

Consider forming a forecast of $\Delta y_{k,t*+1}^{h}$ using information available through $t*$ based on the general model given by Equation (4.1):

$$(4.2) \quad \Delta \hat{y}_{k,t*+h}^{h} = \hat{a}_{k,t*} + \hat{b}_{k,t*} \Delta y_{k,t*} + \sum_{i=1}^{N} \hat{c}_{k,i,t*} x_{i,t*} ,$$

where $\hat{a}_{k,t*}$, $\hat{b}_{k,t*}$, and $\hat{c}_{k,i,t*}$ $(i = 1, \ldots, N)$ are ordinary least square (OLS) estimates of the corresponding parameters in Equation (4.1) based on data from the beginning of the sample through $t*$. When N is large, a serious drawback to this approach is that it can entail substantial in-sample overfitting, which translates into very poor out-of-sample forecasting performance. Intuitively, a highly parameterized model—a model with many $x_{i,t}$ variables—can deliver a substantial R^2 statistic for the in-sample period, but because of model uncertainty and structural instability, the good fit is specific to the sample and not robust.

Goyal and Welch (2008) and Rapach, Strauss, and Zhou (2010) provide recent examples of the poor forecasting performance of kitchen-sink models in the context of forecasting U.S. stock returns. Many potential predictors of aggregate market returns have been proposed in the finance literature, and different theoretical models emphasize different predictors. Goyal and Welch, as well as and Rapach, Strauss, and Zhou, find that general models with a large number of potential predictors from the literature substantially underperform when measured against the simple random-walk model with respect to U.S. stock returns. This type of result is common in the literature, so one can conclude that very simple models are almost always better than very general models for forecasting purposes. When forecasting RIL variables, one should thus avoid kitchen-sink models.[4]

GETS-Bagging

Pretesting provides a method for paring down Equation (4.1) into a more parsimonious model that includes only the important predictors of $\Delta y_{k,t+h}^h$. This is often referred to as general-to-specific (GETS) modeling. Consider again the problem of forming a forecast of $\Delta y_{k,t^*+h}^h$ using information available through t^*. Instead of including all N of the $x_{i,t}$ variables in the forecasting model, as in Equation (4.2), we first estimate Equation (4.1) and compute the t-statistic associated with each $x_{i,t}$. We then drop any variable from the forecasting model with a t-statistic whose absolute value is below a certain threshold, for example, 1.96 or 1.645. The forecasting model thus becomes a reduced version of Equation (4.2) that contains only the significant predictors. In this way, we attempt to identify a more parsimonious forecasting model that only includes what we deem to be important determinants of $\Delta y_{k,t+h}^h$.

While pretesting reduces the dimension of the forecasting model, the selection of the predictors to include in the forecasting model can be sample-specific, thereby representing in-sample overfitting in another guise. Breiman (1996) introduces the idea of bootstrap aggregating (bagging) as a procedure for stabilizing the pretesting decision rule. In essence, we harness the power of the computer to generate a large number of pseudo samples of observations for $\Delta y_{k,t+h}^h$ and $x_{i,t}$ $(i = 1, \ldots, N)$

using bootstrapping techniques. For each pseudo sample, we apply the decision rule and select the predictors to include in the forecasting model, forming a forecast based on the selected predictors under the pseudo sample. The GETS-bagging forecast is then a simple average of the forecasts corresponding to each of the pseudo samples. Intuitively, the pseudo samples provide new learning sets for the decision rule, thereby reducing the instability of the decision rule and its dependence on a specific sample and improving forecasting performance.[5]

Inoue and Kilian (2008) were the first to employ GETS-bagging in a macroeconomic forecasting context (the U.S. inflation rate). They find that GETS-bagging produces significant forecasting gains relative to a simple autoregressive (AR) time-series model and a general model similar to Equation (4.1), as well as relative to pretesting without bagging. More to the theme of this chapter, Rapach and Strauss (forthcoming) find that GETS-bagging produces consistent and significant out-of-sample gains for forecasting U.S. state-level employment growth. Results for forecasting Michigan and Missouri employment growth are discussed in more detail in the next section.

Forecast Combination

Instead of beginning with a general model, forecast combination takes a weighted average of forecasts generated by a large number of individual models. In the context of macroeconomic forecasting, Stock and Watson (1999, 2003, 2004) have popularized a combination approach that pools information from N individual autoregressive distributed lag (ARDL) models:

$$(4.3) \quad \Delta y_{k,t+h}^{h} = a_k + b_k \Delta y_{k,t} + c_{k,i} x_{i,t} + e_{k,t+h}^{h} \quad (i = 1, \ldots, N).$$

Analogous to Equation (4.2), we can form a forecast of $\Delta y_{k,t^*+h}^{h}$ at t^* for each ARDL based on estimates of the parameters in Equation (4.3) derived from data available through t^*.[6] A combination forecast of $\Delta y_{k,t^*+h}^{h}$ is then given by

$$(4.4) \quad \Delta \hat{y}_{k,t^*+h}^{h,C} = \sum_{i=1}^{N} \omega_{i,t^*} \Delta \hat{y}_{k,t^*+h}^{h,i},$$

where $\Delta\hat{y}^{h,i}_{k,t^*+h}$ $(i = 1,\ldots,N)$ is the forecast of $\Delta y^{h}_{k,t^*+h}$ based on the individual ARDL model with $x_{i,t}$, ω_{i,t^*} $(i = 1,\ldots,N)$ is the combining weight corresponding to $\Delta\hat{y}^{h,i}_{k,t^*+h}$, and $\sum_{i=1}^{N}\omega_{i,t^*} = 1$. As stressed by Timmermann (2006), the intuition behind forecast combination is the same as that behind portfolio diversification: we reduce forecasting "risk" by averaging across a large number of individual forecasts, rather than by relying on a single forecasting model.

To implement the combination forecast, we need to determine the combining weights. There are a myriad of methods available for doing this, which are nicely surveyed by Timmermann (2006). An interesting result from the literature is that relatively simple schemes typically outperform more elaborate schemes, even though more elaborate schemes are theoretically optimal under certain assumptions. The problem is that model uncertainty and instability frequently render these assumptions inaccurate, limiting the usefulness of theoretically optimal weights in practice.

A simple combining scheme that often works well in practice is equal weighting: $\omega_{i,t^*} = 1/N$ for all i. In the context of the general model, Equation (4.1), Rapach, Strauss, and Zhou (2010) show that equal weighting can be viewed as a type of "shrinkage" estimator. Intuitively, shrinkage limits the parameter space and prevents overfitting, thereby improving out-of-sample forecasting performance. While equal weighting often produces very consistent forecasting gains, additional gains can be realized by "tilting" the combining weights toward particular individual forecasts. For example, we could select the combining weights based on the performance of the individual forecasting models over a reasonably long holdout out-of-sample test period. The key, however, is not to overdo it. That is, it is typically best to hew fairly closely to equal weighting; otherwise, we have another manifestation of overfitting, and the forecasts become overly susceptible to model uncertainty and instability.[7]

Rapach and Strauss (forthcoming) find that combination forecasts outperform AR benchmark forecasts of U.S. state-level employment growth for 49 of the 50 individual states for a first-quarter 1990 to fourth-quarter 2010 forecast evaluation period, demonstrating the usefulness of the forecast combination approach for RIL variables. Specific results for Michigan and Missouri employment growth forecasts are presented on pp. 59–61.[8] In another recent application, Rapach and

Strauss (2009) show that combination forecasts improve upon AR benchmark forecasts of real housing price growth for a number of interior states for the period from first-quarter 1995 to fourth-quarter 2006. However, combination forecasts do not outperform the AR benchmark forecasts for a number of coastal states during this period, which could indicate that these coastal states experienced housing price bubbles.

Factor Models

Another potentially useful approach for forecasting RIL variables is factor modeling. If RIL variables have strong links to a national variable, factor models can exploit these links to generate improved forecasts. Consider the following simple factor model:

$$(4.5) \quad \Delta y_{k,t} = \alpha_k + \beta_k f_t + \varepsilon_{k,t} \, ,$$

where f_t is an economy-wide or aggregate factor and $\varepsilon_{k,t}$ is a zero-mean disturbance that may be serially correlated. The coefficient on the factor (β_k) is referred to as the factor "loading" or "exposure." This coefficient captures the strength of the relationship between the RIL variable and the aggregate factor, with a larger β_k indicating a stronger response of $\Delta y_{k,t}$ to fluctuations in f_t. Perhaps the best-known example of a factor model in economics and finance is the canonical capital asset pricing model, where $\Delta y_{k,t}$ is the excess return on a particular stock and f_t represents the excess return on the market portfolio. The return on a stock with large β_k value, or "beta," responds more strongly to changes in the market return and thus has greater systemic risk exposure in the context of the capital asset pricing model.[9]

While f_t can be treated as an unobserved latent variable to be estimated (using, e.g., principal component analysis), f_t frequently coincides with an observable aggregate variable. It is then straightforward to construct a forecast of an RIL variable based on Equation (4.5). Consider, for example, forecasting U.S. state-level employment growth using the following factor model specification:

$$(4.6) \quad \Delta \hat{y}_{k,t^*+h}^{h,f} = \hat{\alpha}_{k,t^*} + \hat{\beta}_{k,t^*} \Delta \hat{y}_{US,t^*+h}^h + \hat{\varepsilon}_{k,t^*+h}^h \, ,$$

where $\Delta \hat{y}^h_{US,t*+h}$ is a forecast of aggregate U.S. employment growth; $\hat{\alpha}_{k,t*}$ and $\hat{\beta}_{k,t*}$ are OLS estimates of the intercept and slope coefficients, respectively, in a regression of state k employment growth on U.S. employment growth based on data through $t*$; and $\hat{\varepsilon}^h_{k,t*+h}$ is a forecast of the disturbance term in Equation (4.5) that takes into account the possible serial correlation in the disturbance term.[10] The forecast given by Equation (4.6) requires a forecast of U.S. employment growth to plug into the right-hand side. A GETS-bagging or combination forecast of U.S. employment growth is a natural choice.

Building on Owyang, Rapach, and Wall (2009), Rapach and Strauss (forthcoming) forecast U.S. state-level employment growth using Equation (4.6). They show that factor model forecasts outperform AR benchmark model forecasts for the vast majority of states. The forecasting gains are very sizable for a number of states (including Michigan and Missouri, as described in more detail in the next section). There are a few states, however, where the factor model performs much worse than the AR benchmark, so that factor model forecasts appear to offer gains on a somewhat less consistent basis than GETS-bagging and combination forecasts. Rapach et al. (2011) provide another application in the context of forecasting stock returns for industry-sorted portfolios. They find that a conditional version of the popular Fama-French three-factor model (Fama and French 1993) delivers statistically and economically significant out-of-sample gains for forecasting industry returns.

Estimation Window

The discussion thus far has assumed that the parameters of the forecasting model are estimated using data from the beginning of the available sample through the time of forecast formation. If we suspect the existence of substantial structural breaks, at first blush it may seem appropriate to use an estimation window that excludes prebreak data. As shown by Pesaran and Timmermann (2007) and Clark and McCracken (2009), however, it can be optimal to include prebreak data according to a mean-squared-error criterion; this is a manifestation of the classical bias-efficiency trade-off. Furthermore, Pesaran and Timmermann (2007) and Clark and McCracken (2009) show that the theoretically optimal estimation window is a complicated function of the timing and magnitude of structural breaks. A forecaster will not know these things a priori, so they must be estimated from the data. Estimating the timing of breaks is notoriously difficult. Moreover, by estimating these additional parameters, we again run the risk of having an overly parameterized forecasting model that performs poorly out-of-sample. In practice, it is thus often advisable to employ an expanding window (as assumed in the discussion above). Another strategy is to combine forecasts across models estimated using a variety of window sizes, since this approach recognizes that an expanding window is not necessarily optimal but still avoids the overfitting problem associated with trying to estimate the precise timing of structural breaks.

Amalgamating the Approaches

Finally, it is also worth considering amalgamating the GETS-bagging, forecast combination, and factor model approaches. We can straightforwardly accomplish this by taking an average of the GETS-bagging, combination, and factor model forecasts of an RIL variable. Indeed, Rapach and Strauss (forthcoming) find that such an amalgam forecast performs very well with respect to state-level employment growth: it outperforms the AR benchmark forecast for nearly every state, does not produce the outliers of the factor model approach, and delivers larger gains than the three individual approaches for the clear majority of states. Results for Michigan and Missouri are discussed in the next section.

FORECASTING MICHIGAN AND MISSOURI EMPLOYMENT GROWTH

This section reports more detailed results from Rapach and Strauss (forthcoming) on forecasting Michigan and Missouri state employment growth. The quarterly data composing the full sample span the first quarter of 1976 to the fourth quarter of 2010. Employment data are from the Bureau of Labor Statistics (BLS), and annualized employment growth is computed as 400 times the difference in the log levels of employment. As emphasized in this chapter, there are a host of potential predictors of RIL variables. Rapach and Strauss consider 11 potential predictors, which are given in Table 4.1. These predictors are representative of the types of national and regional determinants of state employment growth suggested by economic intuition and more formal models.[11]

Table 4.1 reports forecasting results for the first-quarter 1990–fourth-quarter 2010 forecast evaluation period and a forecast horizon of two quarters ($h = 2$ in the notation of the previous section). The "AR MSFE" row provides the mean squared forecast error (MSFE) for an AR benchmark model. This is a popular benchmark forecasting model that only relies on lagged values of the variable to be forecasted. While it is a seemingly naive time-series model, such simple time-series models are often difficult to beat in practice. The other rows in Table 4.1 report the ratio of the MSFE for the forecasting model specified in the row heading relative to the AR MSFE. A ratio below (above) unity thus indicates that the competing model outperforms (underperforms) the AR benchmark in terms of MSFE.

As seen in Table 4.1, the AR model produces an MSFE of 4.44 percent (2.57 percent) for Michigan (Missouri). The next rows report MSFE ratios for 11 ARDL models, each based on an individual predictor, as in Equation (4.3). Individual ARDL model results are reported to illustrate the difficulties in identifying a priori the most relevant predictors for a given RIL variable. While all 11 predictors appear plausible, they often vary significantly in their forecasting ability. For example, the ARDL model based on real housing price growth generates an MSFE that is 13 percent higher than the AR benchmark for Michigan, so the AR benchmark provides substantially more accurate forecasts. Housing permit growth, in contrast, reduces MSFE by 6 percent relative to the AR benchmark. In general, as emphasized throughout this chapter, model uncertainty and instability make it extremely difficult to determine a priori the most relevant variables for forecasting RIL variables.[12]

The "GETS-bagging," "Forecast combination," and "Factor model" rows in Table 4.1 report results for the forecasting strategies outlined on pages 54–58.[13] Finally, the "Amalgam" row reports results for an amalgam forecast that takes the form of a simple average of the GETS-bagging, combination, and factor-model forecasts (page 59). Table 4.1 shows that the suggested strategies produce MSFE ratios that are always

Table 4.1 Forecasting Results, State-Level Employment Growth, Two-Quarter Horizon, First-Quarter 1990 to Fourth-Quarter 2010 Evaluation Period

Forecasting model	Michigan	Missouri
AR MSFE	4.44	2.57
ARDL models		
State unemployment rate, differences	1.02	1.01
State real income growth	1.15	1.02
State real housing price growth	1.13	1.02
State housing building permit growth	0.94	1.07
U.S. manufacturing hours, differences	0.99	1.01
U.S. unemployment claims, log levels	0.96	0.79
U.S. new consumer good order growth	0.93	0.83
U.S. building permit growth	0.86	0.93
U.S. real stock price growth	0.82	0.88
U.S. real oil price growth	1.09	1.13
Average adjacent state employment growth	1.08	1.02
Suggested strategies		
GETS-bagging	0.91	0.80
Forecast combination	0.91	0.86
Factor model	0.76	0.65
Amalgam	0.78	0.68

NOTE: The AR (autoregressive) MSFE (mean squared forecast error) row reports the MSFE for the AR benchmark model. Other rows report the MSFE ratio for the forecasting model indicated in the row heading relative to the AR benchmark model.
SOURCE: Adapted from Rapach and Strauss (forthcoming).

below unity, so they consistently deliver forecasting gains relative to the AR benchmark.

Among the GETS-bagging, combination, and factor model forecasts, the factor model forecast performs the best for both Michigan and Missouri. The factor model forecast reduces MSFE by 24 percent (35 percent) relative to the AR benchmark for Michigan (Missouri).[14] For both states, the amalgam forecast also performs well: the MSFE reduction for the amalgam forecast relative to the AR benchmark is a very sizable 22 percent (32 percent) for Michigan (Missouri).

Overall, the results in Table 4.1, together with other results from recent research, illustrate the usefulness of the strategies suggested in this chapter for forecasting RIL variables. Of course, it is important not to read too much into these results and overgeneralize them. Forecasters of RIL variables should thus employ thorough back-testing of these strategies for a given application.[15] Nevertheless, the positive results in recent applications are very promising, so the suggested strategies should form an integral part of a forecaster's toolbox for dealing with the model uncertainty and instability inherent in forecasting RIL variables.

Notes

1. There also may simply be an inadequate number of time-series observations to feasibly estimate a model that includes a very large number of potential predictors.
2. For more extensive coverage of some of the topics covered in this chapter, see the volumes edited by Elliott, Granger, and Timmermann (2006) and Rapach and Wohar (2008), as well as the references at the end of this chapter.
3. The disturbance term will be serially correlated when $h > 1$.
4. Indeed, as mentioned in note 1, OLS estimation of the kitchen-sink model may not even be feasible if the timespan is limited relative to the large number of potential variables that exist for RIL variables.
5. See Inoue and Kilian (2008) and Rapach and Strauss (forthcoming) for more detailed expositions of the construction of bagging forecasts.
6. Again, we can include additional lags of the right-hand-side variables in Equation (4.3) to allow for a more general dynamic structure.
7. Hendry and Clements (2004) provide theoretical insight on how forecast combination can improve forecasting in the presence of structural breaks.
8. Also see Rapach and Strauss (2005), who investigate the performance of a large number of combining methods with respect to forecasting Missouri employment growth.
9. Under the capital asset pricing model, the intercept term should actually be zero in Equation (4.5), since it represents the abnormal, risk-adjusted return (or "alpha"), which will be zero in an efficient market.
10. See Rapach and Strauss (forthcoming) for details on the construction of the disturbance term forecast.
11. Rapach and Strauss (forthcoming) provide data sources for the predictors.
12. In addition, in unreported results, the kitchen-sink model performs very poorly for each state.
13. The combining weights in Equation (4.4) for the combination forecasts are selected based on the performance of the individual models over a relatively long holdout out-of-sample period, as discussed on page 56.
14. With respect to the factor model forecast for Michigan, the average estimate of β_k in Equation (4.5) used in the computation of the factor model forecasts is 1.45,

among the largest for individual U.S. states. Michigan employment thus has large "exposure" to national employment cycles, likely due in large part to the automobile industry's strong link to the national business cycle.

15. Even if back-testing provides positive results, as it says in the fine print, past performance is no guarantee of future success.

References

Breiman, Leo. 1996. "Bagging Predictors." *Machine Learning* 24(2): 123–140.

Clark, Todd E., and Michael W. McCracken. 2009. "Improving Forecast Accuracy by Combining Recursive and Rolling Forecasts." *International Economic Review* 50(2): 363–395.

Elliott, Graham, Clive W.J. Granger, and Allan Timmermann, eds. 2006. *Handbook of Economic Forecasting,* Vol. 1. Amsterdam: North-Holland.

Fama, Eugene F., and Kenneth R. French. 1993. "Common Risk Factors in the Returns on Stocks and Bonds." *Journal of Financial Economics* 33(1): 3–56.

Goyal, Amit, and Ivo Welch. 2008. "A Comprehensive Look at the Empirical Performance of Equity Premium Prediction." *Review of Financial Studies* 21(4): 1455–1508.

Hendry, David F., and Michael P. Clements. 2004. "Pooling of Forecasts." *Econometrics Journal* 7(1): 1–31.

Inoue, Atsushi, and Lutz Kilian. 2008. "How Useful Is Bagging in Forecasting Economic Time Series? A Case Study of U.S. CPI Inflation." *Journal of the American Statistical Association* 103(482): 511–522.

Owyang, Michael T., David E. Rapach, and Howard J. Wall. 2009. "States and the Business Cycle." *Journal of Urban Economics* 65(2): 181–194.

Pesaran, M. Hashem, and Allan Timmermann. 2007. "Selection of Estimation Window in the Presence of Breaks." *Journal of Econometrics* 137(1): 134–161.

Rapach, David E., and Jack K. Strauss. 2005. "Forecasting Employment Growth in Missouri with Many Potentially Relevant Predictors: An Analysis of Forecast Combining Methods." Federal Reserve Bank of St. Louis *Regional Economic Development* 1(1): 97–112.

———. 2009. "Differences in Housing Price Forecastability across U.S. States." *International Journal of Forecasting* 25(2): 351–372.

———. Forthcoming. "Forecasting U.S. State-Level Employment Growth: An Amalgamation Approach." *International Journal of Forecasting.*

Rapach, David E., Jack K. Strauss, Jun Tu, and Guofu Zhou. 2011. "Out-of-

Sample Industry Return Predictability: Evidence from a Large Number of Predictors." Working paper. St. Louis, MO: Saint Louis University, Department of Economics.

Rapach, David E., Jack K. Strauss, and Guofu Zhou. 2010. "Out-of-Sample Equity Premium Prediction: Combination Forecasts and Links to the Real Economy." *Review of Financial Studies* 23(2): 821–862.

Rapach, David E., and Mark E. Wohar, eds. 2008. *Forecasting in the Presence of Structural Breaks and Model Uncertainty*. Frontiers of Economics and Globalization Series, Vol. 3. Bingley, West Yorkshire, UK: Emerald Group Publishing.

Stock, James H., and Mark W. Watson. 1999. "Forecasting Inflation." *Journal of Monetary Economics* 44(2): 293–335.

———. 2003. "Forecasting Output and Inflation: The Role of Asset Prices." *Journal of Economic Literature* 41(3): 788–829.

———. 2004. "Combination Forecasts of Output Growth in a Seven-Country Data Set." *Journal of Forecasting* 23(6): 405–430.

Timmermann, Allan. 2006. "Forecast Combinations." In *Handbook of Economic Forecasting*, Vol. 1, Graham Elliott, Clive W.J. Granger, and Allan Timmermann, eds. Amsterdam: North-Holland, pp. 135–196.

5

Forecasting Asset Prices Using Nonlinear Models

Michael D. Bradley
George Washington University

Dennis W. Jansen
Texas A&M University

Over the past 25 years, a substantial body of research has produced evidence indicating the presence of nonlinearities in the behavior of both financial and real variables. Nonlinearity can arise for a variety of reasons. First, frictions and transaction costs can exceed gains from arbitrage when market deviations are small. Thus, the dynamic reaction to disequilibria may be dependent upon the size of the price change required to restore equilibrium. In other words, transaction costs may be large enough to preclude a complete price response to a small shock but not to large shocks, making the size of the reaction state-dependent.

Another source of nonlinearity is asymmetric dynamics, in which a variable's generating process following declines in its value may differ from the process following increases in its value. For example, the effects of positive shocks may be more persistent than the effects of negative shocks, which may be more rapidly offset. Similarly, herd behavior may cause market participants to overreact during periods of market stress, generating movements in asset prices that exceed normal dynamics. This is another reason a variable's dynamics would be state-dependent.

Still another source of nonlinearity is a variable's volatility. On one level, volatility may be a state variable, with a variable's dynamics changing depending on the state of volatility. Alternatively, volatility itself may be state-dependent, changing because of changes in a state variable such as the state of the economy (expansion, recession) or the state of the financial market (bear market, bull market). These examples show that nonlinearity can arise in the variance or in the mean of the variable. Nonlinearity in the variance typically arises because the variance is time-varying, such as in a generalized autoregressive conditional heteroskedasticity (GARCH) model, whereas nonlinearity in the mean arises because the equation generating the evolution of the mean is nonlinear.

There are a variety of approaches and specific classes of econometric models that have been developed to capture nonlinearities in economic relationships. These include the threshold models (e.g., threshold autoregressive (TAR) models—see Chan and Tong [1986], Tong [1990], and Tsay [1989]); smoothed versions of threshold models (e.g., smooth threshold autoregressive (STAR) models—see Granger and Teräsvirta [1993] and Teräsvirta [1994]); linear models with nonlinear appendages (e.g., the current depth of the recession (CDR) model—see Beaudry and Koop [1993]); the Markov switching model (see Hamilton [1989]); various artificial neural network models (see Cheng and Titterington [1994]); and various nonparametric models in general (see Li and Racine [2007]). These various models have all been employed in estimating nonlinear economic relationships, and most have seen some success as forecasting models.

Many of these models have been applied to business cycles. Neftçi (1984) and Falk (1986) ask whether business cycle dynamics are asymmetric. Teräsvirta and Anderson (1992) and Granger, Teräsvirta, and Anderson (1993) apply smooth transition models to capture business cycle nonlinearities including asymmetries. Van Dijk and Franses (1999) add multiple-regime smooth transition models. Beaudry and Koop (1993) take a different approach, which Potter (1995), Pesaran and Potter (1997), Jansen and Oh (1999), and Bradley and Jansen (1997, 2000) follow up on. However, few of these papers look in-depth at forecasting issues.

Even though nonlinear models have been successfully applied to model a wide variety of financial and macroeconomic variables, the results from using those models to forecast has been mixed. Nonlinear models generally improve upon linear models in terms of in-sample forecasting, but they often show little improvement in terms of out-of-sample forecasting. This somewhat disappointing performance has been ascribed to a number of causes. First, the nonlinearity may not occur in the forecast period. The forecasting advantage of a nonlinear model could arise from its ability to accurately capture the dynamics of a series during periods of time when it exhibits nonlinear behavior. If the out-of-sample forecasting period does not include any such periods, there will be no forecasting advantage for the nonlinear model.

This characteristic of nonlinear models to capture periods of time with "normal" dynamics as well as with exceptional dynamics can lead to other forecasting issues. One such issue is the need to forecast the regime switch or structural break in which the dynamics change. In an out-of-sample forecast, the moment of switch is unknown and may in itself be difficult to forecast, thus reducing the utility of the nonlinear model. Similarly, nonlinear forecasts may be state-dependent, meaning that an accurate out-of-sample forecast will require accurate forecasts of the state of nature over the period of the forecast. For linear models the impact of a shock is the same regardless of the state of the world in which the shock occurs. For nonlinear models this is not true—a disturbance or shock will have different impacts depending on the state of the world in which the shock occurs. Finally, if periods with exceptional dynamics are relatively rare but empirically significant, there may be a tendency for nonlinear models to overfit the sample, reducing their value in an out-of-sample forecast.

A last challenge for out-of-sample forecasting comes from the difficulties in using nonlinear models in multistep forecasts. Linear models can be solved recursively, making the calculation of multistep forecasts relatively straightforward. This is not true for nonlinear models. The nonlinearity makes multiple-step-ahead forecasting intrinsically more difficult. We will outline some of the difficulties with multiple-step-ahead forecasts later in this paper.

These problems notwithstanding, we believe it is important to continue the research into nonlinear forecasts so we can make better use of our ability to model the nonlinear aspects of the economy. We find the problems not to be drawbacks of nonlinear models so much as challenges that must be overcome to improve the accuracy of forecasts. The problems lead to inaccuracy in both linear and nonlinear forecasts, and the task is to better understand nonlinear forecasting in order to overcome these obstacles.

We thus examine an ongoing research question as to whether financial-sector variables help forecast real-sector variables, or real-sector variables help forecast financial sector variables—or both. We use nonlinear models to investigate this question. We do so because this allows us to investigate the out-of-sample forecasting ability of these nonlinear models in a multivariate context.

THEORETICAL PRELIMINARIES

The specific relationship that we investigate is between a key cyclical real-sector variable (industrial production) and two financial-sector variables, the 10-year Treasury bond rate and excess returns for Standard and Poor's 500. We model that relationship using nonlinear approaches and then examine the out-of-sample forecasting properties of those models. Before estimating the models and evaluating the forecasts we present three important definitions and a description of the data we use. What follows here is just the briefest of introductions to ideas of financial economics that provide the backdrop to any financial forecasting exercise.

The first definition is the asset pricing equation. A typical first-order condition from an asset allocation problem (i.e., a typical Euler equation for an asset pricing problem) is found in Equation (5.1):

$$(5.1) \quad u'(c_t) = \beta E_t \left[u'(c_{t+1}) R_{t+1} \right] ,$$

where $u(c_t)$ is a utility function, $u'(c_t)$ indicates the derivative of the utility function, R_{t+1} is real gross return on stocks purchased at time t and held until time $t + 1$, and c_t is real consumption at time t. Typically, optimization requires equating the marginal utility of current consumption (the left-hand side of Equation [5.1]) to the marginal utility of deferring consumption to the next period (the right-hand side of Equation [5.1]). The marginal utility of current consumption is straightforward and is written as $u'(c_t)$. The marginal utility of deferring consumption to the next period is calculated as the product of three terms: 1) the rate of return on a unit of deferred consumption, R_{t+1}; 2) the marginal utility of consumption that is deferred to the next period, $u'(c_{t+1})$; and 3) the discount factor β (used to calculate the present value of this additional future marginal utility).

Equation (5.1) is potentially highly nonlinear, and any variable affecting consumption can potentially affect forecasts of stock returns. This asset pricing condition provides a theoretical basis for nonlinear econometric modeling.

The second definition is of excess returns. Common models of equity returns focus on modeling excess returns, which are returns over and above a risk premium. Often the risk premium is a government bond yield, in which case excess returns are returns on equity over and above returns on the government bond. We thus define excess returns as

$$(5.2) \quad ER_{t+1} = \frac{S_{t+1} + D_{t+1}}{S_t} - I_t = R_{t+1} - I_t .$$

Here, ER_{t+1} is the excess return on stocks purchased at time t and held until time $t + 1$, and R_{t+1} is the gross return on stocks purchased at time t and held until time $t + 1$. The gross return on bonds purchased at time t and held until time $t + 1$ is I_t.

The third and last definition is that of the information set used for forecasting. It is important to think carefully about what should be included in the information set when investigating the forecasting performance of various models. The excess return formula indicates that, at time t, an investor knows the nominal return on bonds between t and $t + 1$. If one were to buy a bond at time t, one would know what its interest payments were between t and $t + 1$. But when one buys equity, one won't know the equity's return between t and $t + 1$ until time $t + 1$ occurs and one can observe the price of stock at time $t + 1$. With this definition of the information set, Ω, we can define the forecast for an excess return as

$$(5.3) \quad E(ER_{t+1} \mid \Omega_t) = E\left(\frac{S_{t+1} + D_{t+1}}{S_t} \mid \Omega_t \right) - I_t .$$

DATA DESCRIPTION

We estimate models of excess returns on equities and bond interest rates using monthly data for the United States. The two sources for our data are 1) Shiller's monthly data set on stocks and associated variables and 2) Federal Reserve System data on industrial production. We also employ a measure of the general price level, the Consumer Price Index calculated by the Bureau of Labor Statistics.

Our data include the value of the Standard and Poor's (S&P) 500 index at the end of each month, calculated as the monthly average of daily closing prices. We represent this variable as the stock index value S_t. Dividends are represented by the symbol D_t, and according to Shiller

(2011) are "computed from the S&P four-quarter tools for the quarter since 1926, with linear interpolation to monthly figures." The price index, P_t, is the CPI-U series. Industrial production is y_t. Finally, we use Shiller's 10-year government security rate (GS10) as our measure of the gross long-term nominal interest rate, I_t.

Below are plots of the key variables. Figure 5.1 graphs the log of industrial production (left scale) and the growth rate, calculated as changes in the log of industrial production (right scale). The general upward trend in industrial production is clearly visible, as are various periods when industrial production was declining. These periods are typically recessions, such as the period around 1975 and the period at the end of our sample, 2009. The plot of the growth rate indicates periods of greater volatility, especially at the beginning of our sample, 1955–1960, and again at the end of our sample. The impact of the recession in 1974–1975 is clear. The long period of relatively low volatility in the growth rate of industrial production from the mid-1980s until 2005 is also apparent.

Figure 5.1 U.S. Industrial Production, January 1955–December 2009

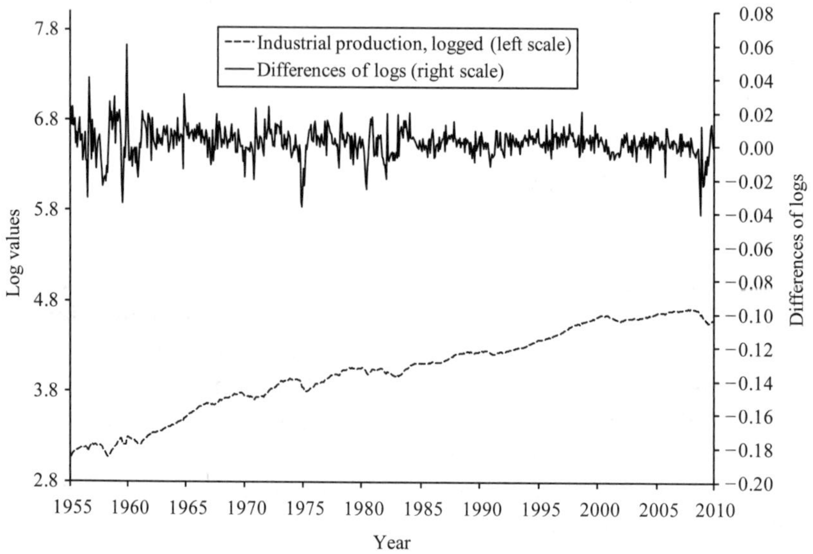

SOURCE: Authors' calculations.

Figure 5.2 graphs the log of the stock price index, both its level (left-hand scale) and its growth rate (right-hand scale). Again the general upward trend in the stock price index is clear, as are periods of declining stock prices after 2000 and again at the end of our sample. The growth rate of stock prices shows considerably more volatility than the growth rate of industrial production. For stock prices, monthly changes of plus or minus 0.1 (10 percent) occur at times, whereas we do not see such large movements in industrial production.

Figure 5.3 graphs our interest rate data, where we have converted this series to monthly net interest rates. Interest rate levels are shown on the left-hand scale, while changes in the interest rate levels, calculated as simple differences, are shown on the right-hand scale. Most apparent is the secular increase in interest rates from the beginning of our sample until the very early 1980s, and the secular decline from the early 1980s until the end of our sample. Interest rates begin our sample at about 0.2 percent per month (roughly 2.4 percent per year), increase to a rate of

Figure 5.2   U.S. Stock Price Index, January 1955–December 2009

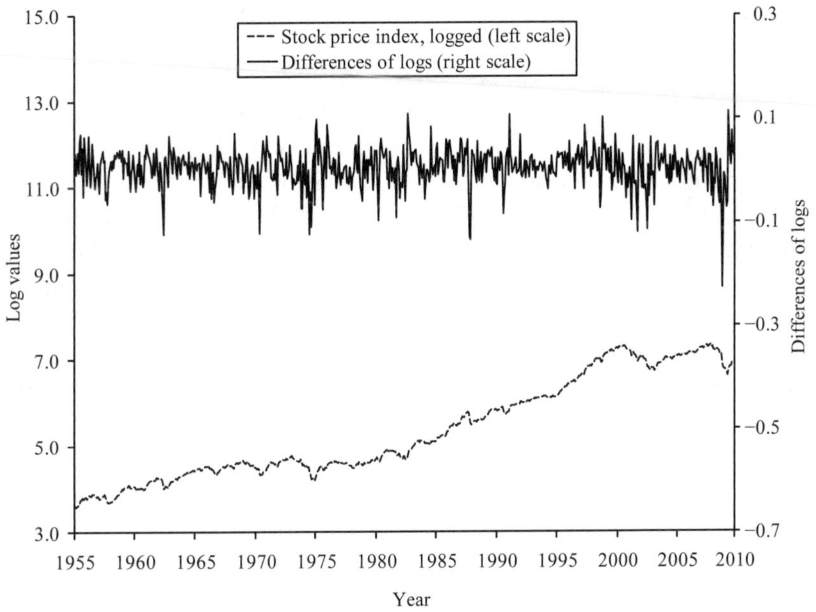

SOURCE: Authors' calculations.

Figure 5.3 U.S. Interest Rate, January 1955–December 2009

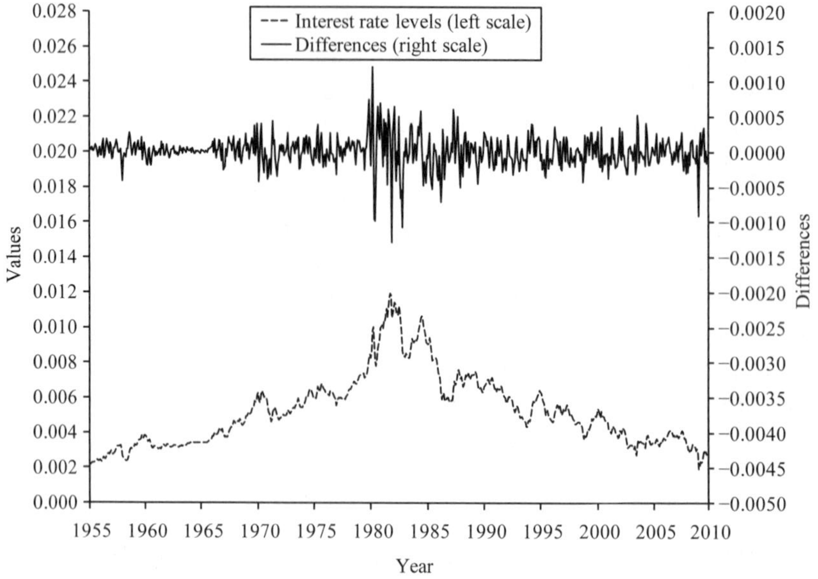

SOURCE: Authors' calculations.

almost 1.2 percent per month (roughly 14.4 percent per year), and then return by the end of our sample to a rate near 0.2 percent per month. This run-up and subsequent decline in rates is most often blamed on inflation rates, which increased from the mid-1960s through the 1970s, peaking in the early 1980s before declining gradually throughout the next several decades. Of course, the large secular movements contain many shorter periods of ups and downs in interest rates, as the graph of interest rate changes makes clear. Also apparent in the graph of interest rate changes is the high volatility from the late 1970s through the early 1980s.

ESTIMATING THE NONLINEAR MODELS

In this section we describe how we estimate the nonlinear models that we use for producing our out-of-sample forecasts. Our estimation proceeds in three steps. First we test for linearity in our three variables. The null hypothesis will be that the modeled relationship is linear, and a rejection leads to continued estimation of a nonlinear model. The idea is not to estimate a nonlinear model if that is unnecessary. Second, when nonlinearity is detected, we will estimate a threshold model. Third, we will also estimate a second nonlinear model, which we will call a "current depth of recession" model.

Threshold models capture the possibility that the dynamics of a variable may be state-dependent. They allow the data-generating process to vary across two or more states of nature. For this reason, they are also often called "regime-switching" models. Seasonal models for industrial production or "day of week" models for stock returns are examples of *deterministic* threshold models. For these models the occurrence of a regime switch is known with certainty. However, many interesting cases involve *stochastic* threshold models, in which the regime switch is unknown. An example is given by a model in which stock market returns are driven by a different dynamic process after large declines in stock prices. Bradley and Jansen (2004) provide one attempt at forecasting stock returns in a nonlinear framework.

Threshold models are an example of a model in which the state variable is observable. In a deterministic threshold model it is clear that we observe the day of the week and that we can allow our model to behave differently on different days of the week. In a stochastic threshold model we can observe that there has been a large decline in stock prices, and then we can allow our model to behave differently after such a large decline. The key feature is that the state variable, either the day of the week or the decline in stock prices, is observable. This stands in contrast to models with unobserved state variables, such as the various Markov switching models. In those models the state variable is an unobserved variable, and changes in the underlying hidden state variable lead to changes in the behavior of the variable we are modeling. Thus a key modeling decision is between using a nonlinear model with observable state variables and using a nonlinear model with hidden or unobserved state variables. The choice depends in part on whether there are observed variables that can adequately indicate or represent the state of the world. Here we estimate and forecast with observable state variables.

We investigate two types of threshold models, the threshold autoregressive (TAR) model and the smooth transition autoregressive (STAR) model. A TAR model specifies (at least) two sets of dynamics for the variable of interest, y, with the regime switch dependent upon the value of a "transition" variable, labeled z. The threshold model can be written as follows:

$$y_t = a_0 + \sum_{i=1}^{p} \alpha_i y_{t-i} + \left(\sum_{i=1}^{p} \beta_i y_{t-i} \right) \delta_t + \varepsilon_t ,$$

where

$$(5.4) \quad \delta_t = \begin{cases} 0 \text{ if } z_{t-d} \leq c \\ \\ 1 \text{ if } z_{t-d} > c . \end{cases}$$

In this threshold model, the behavior of the variable y_t is a pth order autoregressive model governed by the coefficients α_i when the transition variable z_{t-d} is below the threshold value, c. When the transition variable is greater than the threshold value, the behavior of the variable y_t is an autoregressive model governed by the coefficients $\alpha_i + \beta_i$. Thus the variable y_t changes behavior depending on the relationship between the transition variable and the threshold.

The transition variable is the observable state variable we mentioned above. Changes in this variable lead to changes in the behavior of y_t. The transition variable has a subscript $t - d$ to indicate that it is a lagged value, and d is an integer value of 1 or higher. The parameter d is known as the "delay" and indicates the delay between changes in the transition variable and changes in the behavior of y_t.

The TAR model seems simple, with an indicator variable δ switching from zero to one as the transition variable crosses a threshold value. This is a step function, with δ equaling zero when z_{t-d} is on one side of the threshold and one when z_{t-d} is on the other side of the threshold. Yet, despite this simplicity, the TAR model has proven useful as a model to capture nonlinear behavior.

The STAR model generalizes the threshold approach by allowing a smooth transition between the two regimes. This transition is governed by a function of the threshold variable, z, and the transition function is usually specified as being either logistic (LSTAR) or exponential (ESTAR). The shape of the transition function governs the nature of the movement from one regime to another. The main difference is that logistic specification is one-sided, in the sense that there are alternative dynamics for either large or small values of the transition function, and an intermediate range where the dynamics are a combination of the dynamics at the two extremes. The exponential specification is two-sided, in the sense that there is a set of dynamics for both large and small values, and a different set of dynamics for intermediate values.

The structure of the STAR model is given by

$$ y_t \;=\; a_0 \;+\; \sum_{i=1}^{p} \alpha_i y_{t-i} + \left(\sum_{i=1}^{p} \beta_i y_{t-i} \right) F(z_{t-d}) + \varepsilon_t \;, $$

where

$$ (5.5) \quad F(z_{t-d}) \;=\; \left[1 + e^{-\gamma(z_{t-d} - c)} \right]^{-1} \qquad \text{(LSTAR)} $$

or

$$ F(z_{t-d}) \;=\; \left[1 - e^{-\gamma(z_{t-d} - c)^{\wedge 2}} \right], \gamma > 0 \qquad \text{(ESTAR).} $$

We illustrate the nature of a STAR model transition function in Figure 5.4. In a TAR model there is a discrete switch between the two regimes, as illustrated by the line that goes almost straight up. The transition function takes a value of zero before the period of the switch and a value of one afterward. In a STAR model the switch between the regimes is more gradual, with the degree of smoothness depending upon the size of the transition parameter, γ. When gamma takes a small value the transition is very gradual, as illustrated by the dotted line. As gamma gets larger, the STAR model begins to approximate the discrete switch of the TAR model, as illustrated by the curved lighter line. Thus, one advantage of the STAR model is that it permits, but does not require, a relatively abrupt switch between regimes.

There are four steps involved in identifying and estimating a STAR model. The first step is the identification and estimation of a linear auto-

Figure 5.4 STAR Transition Functions—Role of Gamma

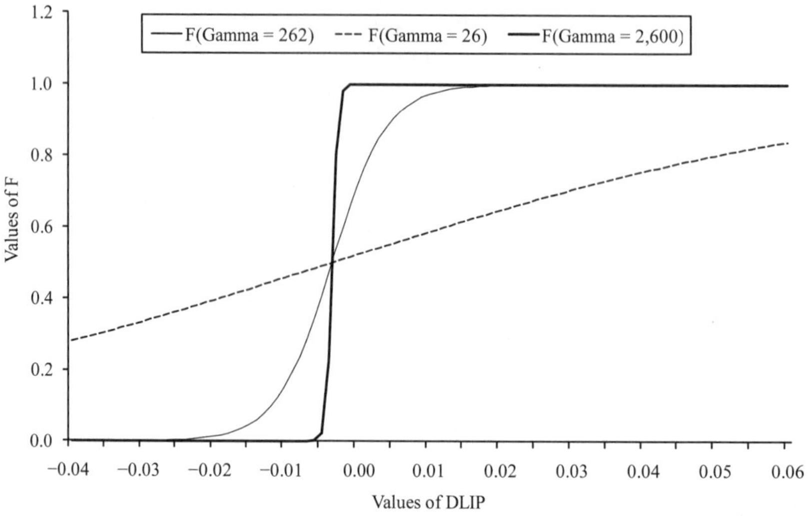

SOURCE: Authors' calculations.

regressive model. The primary purpose of this step is to determine the lag lengths that will be used for linearity testing and, if nonlinearity is detected, for estimating the STAR model. Step two is to test for linearity, to make sure that a nonlinear model is needed. If linearity is not rejected, there is often no need to continue the process of estimating a nonlinear model. If linearity *is* rejected, the third step is to identify the STAR model specification. Here identification is used in the time series sense and is meant to specify the various features of the model, such as lag lengths. It is in this third step that one determines whether an exponential or a logistical star model is appropriate. The last step is the actual estimation of the specified STAR model. This can be done with various nonlinear optimization procedures, and we use nonlinear least squares.

In this exercise we will identify and estimate three models: one for industrial production, one for a long-term bond rate, and one for excess equity returns. We begin the estimation of the linear models with stationarity testing. We perform both the Augmented Dickey-Fuller (ADF) and the Kwiatkowski-Phillips-Schmidt-Shin (KPSS) tests, and the results are presented in Table 5.1. Note that the ADF test has a null hypothesis of nonstationarity or "integrated of order one," written as I(1). The KPSS test has a null hypothesis of stationarity, or I(0).

Our ADF tests fail to reject the null of I(1) for the levels of the log industrial production [Log(IP)] and the bond interest rate (INT), but reject that null for the level of excess returns (ER). This indicates that log industrial production and the bond interest rate should be differenced, while excess returns are stationary as calculated. We note that the ADF test fails to reject the null of I(1) for the S&P 500, which is consistent with the result that excess returns, calculated in part from differencing the log S&P 500 index [Log(S)], are I(0). The ADF results are corroborated by the KPSS tests, which reject the null of I(0) for the levels of the log of industrial production and the bond rate, but fail to reject that null for excess returns.

Table 5.1 Testing for Stationarity

Variable	ADF test[a] series in levels	ADF test[a] series in first differences	KPSS test[b] series in levels	KPSS test[b] series in first differences
Log(IP)	−2.55	−12.25	0.42	0.14
	($p = 0.31$)	(0.00)	(5% CV = 0.15)	(5% CV = 0.46)
	(2 lags, trend)	(1 lag)	(trend)	
	Fail to reject	Reject	Reject	Fail to reject
Log(S)	−1.71	−19.29	0.63	0.10
	($p = 0.75$)	($p = 0.00$)	(5% CV = 0.15)	(5% CV = 0.46)
	(1 lag, trend)	(0 lags)	(trend)	
	Fail to reject	Reject	Reject	Fail to reject
INT	−1.73	−18.08	0.96	0.27
	($p = 0.42$)	(0.00)	(5% CV = 0.15)	(5% CV = 0.46)
	(2 lags)	(1 lag)		
	Fail to reject	Reject	Reject	Fail to reject
ER	−19.20		0.09	
	($p = 0.00$)		(5% CV = 0.15)	
	(0 lags)			
	Reject		Fail to reject	

NOTE: Blank = not applicable.
[a] ADF test: Null hypothesis is I(1).
[b] KPSS test: Null hypothesis is I(0).
SOURCE: Authors' calculations.

Based upon these two tests, we estimate linear models in the first differences of the log of industrial production (DLIP) and the bond interest rate (DINT), and in the level of excess returns (ER). We proceed to determine the appropriate lag length for these linear models, and here we select the lag lengths using a standard goodness of fit criterion, the Schwartz Information Criterion (SIC). Using the SIC to pick lag lengths involves searching over a range of possible lag lengths selected a priori and finding the lag length within that set that will minimize the SIC. Here we searched over a range from 1 lag to 12 lags.

Our models will possibly contain multiple right-hand-side variables at various lags, and not just lags of the dependent variable. This raises a few issues with lag selection. One procedure is to search over the entire lag space, with 1 through 12 lags of each variable. If there are three right-hand-side variables, as there are in some of our models, this involves 12 cubed regressions. An alternative is to use an iterative procedure, first picking the lags of the dependent variable and then proceeding with the other explanatory variables. We follow this latter approach. We first selected the best univariate model, then the best lags of the second variable, holding constant the lags specified for the dependent variable in the univariate specification, and then the best lags of the third variable given the lags of the first two variables. The results are provided in Table 5.2.

The linear model for the change in the log of industrial production contains two lags of the change in the log of industrial production, two lags of excess stock returns, and one lag of the change in the interest rate. The linear models for the asset returns are more parsimonious. Neither one contains any lags of change of the log of industrial production, so the real sector variable will not be included in the models for the financial variables.

Table 5.2 Determining the Lag Length for the Linear Models

	DLIP	ER	DINT
Univariate	AR(2); −6.74	AR(1); −3.93	AR(2); −14.14
Bivariate	2 lags ER; −6.75	0 lags DLIP; −3.93	2 lags ER; −14.15
Trivariate	1 lag DINT; −6.75	1 lag DINT; −3.94	0 lags DLIP; −14.15

SOURCE: Authors' calculations.

The estimated linear models are presented in Table 5.3. Estimation was by ordinary least squares. Excess returns have a positive effect on current growth in industrial production. Interestingly, increases in the interest rate also have a positive effect on current growth in industrial production. As for excess returns, increases in the interest rate have a decidedly negative impact on excess returns. Finally, changes in the interest rate are affected positively by excess returns.

The next step is to test for linearity. We use the approach derived by Luukkonen, Saikkonen, and Teräsvirta (1988) and Teräsvirta and

Table 5.3 Linear Model Estimates

	DLIP	ER	DINT
Constant	0.0015	4.43E-04	1.20E-06
	(0.0004)	(1.36E-03)	(8.18E-06)
	$p = 0.0000$	$p = 0.7440$	$p = 0.8829$
DLIP(−1)	0.3098	—	—
	(0.0404)	—	—
	$p = 0.0000$	—	—
DLIP(−2)	0.1028	—	—
	(0.0399)	—	—
	$p = 0.0103$	—	—
ER(−1)	0.0231	0.2086	6.27E-04
	(0.0100)	(0.0397)	(2.50E-4)
	$p = 0.0211$	$p = 0.0000$	$p = 0.0122$
ER(−2)	0.0308	—	6.31E-04
	(0.0099)	—	(2.50E-04)
	$p = 0.0020$	—	$p = 0.0119$
DINT(−1)	4.6626	−26.5785	0.3863
	(1.5652)	(6.2857)	(0.0404)
	$p = 0.0030$	$p = 0.0000$	$p = 0.0000$
DINT(−2)	—	—	−0.1925
	—	—	(0.0406)
	—	—	$p = 0.0122$
R^2	0.1951	0.0842	0.1720
Std. error	0.0081	0.0332	0.0002
SIC	−6.7509	−3.9441	−14.1487

NOTE: — = data not available.
SOURCE: Authors' calculations.

Anderson (1992), in which linearity is tested with the "approximating equation." The advantage of this approach is that it simultaneously tests for linearity and provides guidance about the specification of the non-linear model. The approximating equation is given as follows:

$$(5.6) \quad y_t = \beta_0 + \sum_{i=1}^{p} \beta_{1,i} y_{t-i} + \sum_{i=1}^{p} \beta_{2,i} y_{t-i} z_{t-d} + \sum_{i=1}^{p} \beta_{3,i} y_{t-i} z_{t-d}^2$$

$$+ \sum_{i=1}^{p} \beta_{4,i} y_{t-i} z_{t-d}^3 + \varepsilon_t \ ,$$

where y_t is the variable being modeled, z_{t-d} is the transition variable, and d is the delay between when the transition variable crosses the threshold value and the variable of interest's alternative dynamics become active. The null hypothesis of linearity is a test of $\beta_{2i} = \beta_{3i} = \beta_{4i} = 0$.

We take a general approach to testing for linearity by using five possible transition variables and up to a three-period delay. We start by using the dependent variable as the transition variable to see if the variable's own values indicate the source of nonlinearity. This would mean, for example, that the change in the log of the industrial production would be the transition variable for itself. We then look at the possibility that one of the other two variables being modeled could be the transition variable. For the change in the log of industrial production, this means testing whether the change in the bond rate or excess returns is the transition variable. Finally, we consider two external variables. The first, called current depth of the recession, or CDR, is the distance from the past peak in industrial production and its current value. This variable would capture a situation in which recessions and expansions had alternative dynamics. A variable similarly defined for the stock index, CDB (current depth of stocks), measures the difference between the previous peak in the S&P 500 index and index's current value. This variable would capture a situation in which rising and falling S&P 500 index values generated different dynamics.

The results of estimating the approximating equation and testing for linearity are given in Table 5.4. First, there is no evidence suggesting rejection of linearity for excess returns. No tests for any threshold variable for any delay are close to suggesting a rejection of linearity. We conclude that excess returns are best modeled here as a linear process. There is abundant evidence, however, to support rejecting

Table 5.4 Testing for Linearity

Threshold variables	Dependent variables for linearity test					
	DLIP		ER		DINT	
	Chi-sq.	P-value	Chi-sq.	P-value	Chi-sq.	P-value
CDB(−1)	35.59	0.0020	5.03	0.5402	18.27	0.1076
CDR(−1)	30.63	0.0098	4.34	0.6302	28.47	0.0047
ER(−1)	22.08	0.1056	2.43	0.8764	52.13**	0.0000
DINT(−1)	16.59	0.3442	8.68	0.1925	51.96*	0.0000
DLIP(−1)	52.25**	0.0001	8.77	0.1871	25.80	0.0114
CDB(−2)	41.87*	0.0002	2.73	0.8424	20.88	0.0522
CDR(−2)	28.53	0.0185	7.91	0.2445	30.83	0.0021
ER(−2)	29.70	0.0131	5.36	0.4985	24.30	0.0185
DINT(−2)	17.23	0.3052	6.83	0.3369	43.54	0.0000
DLIP(−2)	25.84	0.0398	5.03	0.5400	19.52	0.0768
CDB(−3)	29.04	0.0159	1.68	0.9467	15.93	0.1944
CDR(−3)	14.45	0.4917	5.75	0.4515	35.18	0.0004
ER(−3)	19.50	0.1921	5.20	0.5182	39.93	0.0001
DINT(−3)	31.66	0.0072	3.48	0.7469	40.05	0.0001
DLIP(−3)	17.54	0.2878	6.50	0.3692	9.66	0.6459

NOTE: * significant at the 0.10 level (two-tailed test); ** significant at the 0.05 level (two-tailed test).

SOURCE: Authors' calculations.

linearity for both the change in the log of industrial production and the change in the bond rate. Of the 15 different tests for linearity, 9 of them support rejection, suggesting that a finding of nonlinearity is not dependent upon a very specific combination of threshold variable and delay. A review of all instances that show rejection indicates that a single lag of the change in the log of industrial production should be chosen as the threshold variable. Similar results are found for the change in the bond rate, in that 11 of the 15 tests produce evidence indicating rejection of linearity. A review of those tests indicates that a single lag of excess returns should be chosen as the threshold variable for the change in the bond rate.

Given that we find evidence rejecting linearity for two of the variables, the next step is to identify which STAR model is appropriate for each, the LSTAR or the ESTAR model. This is done through a series of hypothesis tests on the coefficients in the approximating equation. The null hypothesis of linearity is tested through setting to zero all of the estimated coefficients on the threshold variable. The identification of the model specification looks at similar tests for subsets of the coefficients. Teräsvirta and Anderson (1992) specify a set of three hypotheses:

(5.7) $\quad H_1 : \beta_{4,i} = 0, \forall i$,

$\quad H_2 : \beta_{3,i} = 0 \mid \beta_{4,i} = 0, \forall i$, and

$\quad H_3 : \beta_{2,i} = 0 \mid \beta_{3,i} = \beta_{4,i} = 0, \forall i$.

Rejection of H_1 indicates that an LSTAR model is appropriate. Failure to reject H_1 but rejection of H_2 indicates that an ESTAR model is appropriate. Finally, failure to reject H_1 or H_2 but rejection of H_3 indicates that an LSTAR model is appropriate.

The results of testing theses hypotheses for our models are presented in Table 5.5. The table shows that H_1 is rejected for both variables, indicating an LSTAR specification is appropriate for both the change in the log of industrial production and the change in the bond rate.

At this point we estimated the LSTAR model for changes in the log of industrial production by nonlinear least squares, with results reported in Table 5.6. There are some important issues in estimating TAR and STAR models that have to do with discontinuities in the likelihood function, and these have been documented and discussed in Hansen (1997). Our solution is to conduct a grid search for various values of the threshold value in the TAR model, and the parameter estimates of the TAR model are used as starting values for the STAR estimation.

In Table 5.6 we will first examine the transition variable and its role in our model. The transition variable is one lag of the change in the log of industrial production. Here the estimated value for the threshold is −0.0035, which suggests that, roughly, the dynamics of the growth in industrial production will differ when that growth is positive (specifically, above −0.0035) as compared to when it is negative (specifically, below −0.0035).

Table 5.5 Identifying the STAR Model Specifications

Hypothesis tests	Dependent variable: DLIP		Dependent variable: DINT	
	Chi-sq.	Prob.	Chi-sq.	Prob.
	Threshold variable: DLIP(−1)		Threshold variable: ER(−1)	
$H_0 : \beta_{2,i} = \beta_{3,i} = \beta_{4,i} = 0, \forall i$	52.25	0.0000	52.13	0.0000
$H_1 : \beta_{4,i} = 0, \forall i$	16.90	0.0047	13.85	0.0078
$H_2 : \beta_{3,i} = 0 \mid \beta_{4,i} = 0, \forall i$	14.01	0.0155	3.14	0.5340
$H_3 : \beta_{2,i} = 0 \mid \beta_{3,i} = \beta_{4,i} = 0, \forall i$	21.34	0.0007	35.13	0.0000
	Threshold variable: CDB(−2)		Threshold variable: DINT(−1)	
$H_0 : \beta_{2,i} = \beta_{3,i} = \beta_{4,i} = 0, \forall i$	41.87	0.0002	51.96	0.0000
$H_1 : \beta_{4,i} = 0, \forall i$	12.79	0.0254	9.91	0.0420
$H_2 : \beta_{3,i} = 0 \mid \beta_{4,i} = 0, \forall i$	2.60	0.7611	17.62	0.0015
$H_3 : \beta_{2,i} = 0 \mid \beta_{3,i} = \beta_{4,i} = 0, \forall i$	26.48	0.0001	24.43	0.0001

SOURCE: Authors' calculations.

One important issue to examine is whether one regime of the STAR model is just being estimated on a single or a very few data points, so that the model is really just showing that a few data points are a special case. To examine this issue we use the following histogram, Figure 5.5, which shows that the estimated threshold does not simply identify a few observations at the extreme tail of the distribution. Instead, we see that, over the history of the variable, many observations occur above, and below, the threshold. Thus both regimes occurred with some regularity.

The estimated value of the transition parameter, γ, is relatively large at 262.04, suggesting a relatively sharp transition between the regimes, as DLIP(−1) varies around −0.0035. We thus also estimate a TAR model for the change in the log of industrial production to serve as a

Table 5.6 LSTAR for DLIP, January 1955–December 2004

Constant	0.0018	(0.0004);	$p = 0.0001$
DLIP(−1)	0.1795	(0.1034);	$p = 0.0830$
DLIP(−2)	0.3527	(0.1265);	$p = 0.0055$
ER(−1)	−0.0116	(0.0313);	$p = 0.7115$
ER(−2)	0.1109	(0.0381);	$p = 0.0037$
DINT(−1)	9.0912	(3.4673);	$p = 0.0090$
DLIP(−1) × F[DLIP(−1)]	0.1581	(0.1325);	$p = 0.2331$
DLIP(−2) × F[DLIP(−1)]	−0.3357	(0.1508);	$p = 0.0263$
ER(−1) × F[DLIP(−1)]	0.0502	(0.0407);	$p = 0.2173$
ER(−2) × F[DLIP(−1)]	−0.1145	(0.0486);	$p = 0.0189$
DINT(−1) × F[DLIP(−1)]	−7.3670	(4.9938);	$p = 0.1407$
Gamma	262.04	(187.44);	$p = 0.1626$
Threshold for DLIP(−1)	−0.0035	(0.0032);	$p = 0.2758$
R^2		0.2283	
Std. error		0.0079	
SIC		−6.7184	
Log likelihood		2,057.110	

SOURCE: Authors' calculations.

basis for comparison with the STAR model. The estimated value for the threshold for the TAR model is reported in Table 5.7 and is very close to that of the STAR model. Figure 5.6 graphs the transition functions for the TAR and STAR model. Of course this is a step function for the TAR model, and, as the graph makes clear for the STAR model, there is a large range where the two extreme regimes are "smoothly" combined to generate the dynamics that we observe. As the following graph shows, the switch between regimes takes place just below zero.

The estimated LSTAR model for the change in the bond rate is presented in Table 5.8. The coefficients on lags of the changes in the bond rate in the lower regime were statistically insignificant in initial estimates of both the STAR and TAR models, and their inclusion caused convergence difficulties for the STAR model, so we set these two coefficients to zero for the results reported in Table 5.8 (and for the TAR model reported in Table 5.9).

Figure 5.5 Histogram for DLIP

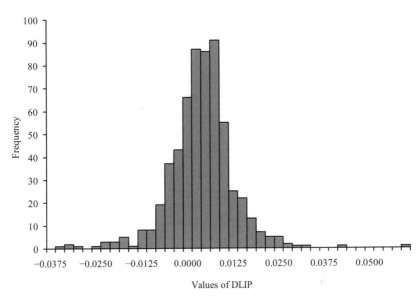

SOURCE: Authors' calculations.

For the bond rate the transition variable is one lag of the change in the bond rate, or DINT(−1). The estimated threshold value is −0.00048, a value that falls far to the left in the distribution of changes in the bond rate between positive and negative values, suggesting that changes in the bond rate are largely governed by one regime, with occasional large declines in the bond rate leading to alternative dynamics. Figure 5.7 presents the histogram of excess returns. We see that there are only a small, though not trivial, number of observations in the lower regime.

The estimated value for the transition parameter is also large for this model, 464.7, so we again estimate a TAR model for comparison, with results reported in Table 5.9. In the TAR model, the estimated threshold value is −0.00048, nearly the same as the STAR model. Given this and the size of the transition variable in the LSTAR model, the two models provide very similar results in terms of the region around the switch, as seen in Figure 5.8.

So far, we have estimated four nonlinear models to be used in out-of-sample forecasting, an LSTAR and a TAR for both the change in

Table 5.7 TAR For DLIP, January 1955–December 2004

Constant	0.0018	(0.0005);	$p = 0.0001$
DLIP(−1)	0.2199	(0.0818);	$p = 0.0074$
DLIP(−2)	0.2635	(0.0823);	$p = 0.0014$
ER(−1)	0.0013	(0.0190);	$p = 0.9461$
ER(−2)	0.0800	(0.0178);	$p = 0.0000$
DINT(−1)	9.3324	(2.6351);	$p = 0.0004$
DLIP(−1) × δ	0.0971	(0.1095);	$p = 0.3755$
DLIP(−2) × δ	−0.2099	(0.0932);	$p = 0.0246$
ER(−1) × δ	0.0303	(0.0222);	$p = 0.1727$
ER(−2) × δ	−0.0679	(0.0213);	$p = 0.0015$
DINT(−1) × δ	−7.1795	(3.2521);	$p = 0.0277$
Threshold for DLIP(−1)		−0.003	
R^2		0.2258	
Std. error		0.0079	
SIC		−6.7365	
Log likelihood		2,056.135	

SOURCE: Authors' calculations.

the log of industrial production and the change in the bond rate. We now supplement these models with an alternative approach to capturing nonlinearity among the real and financial variables. We specify and estimate CDR models for the change in the log of industrial production, for excess returns, and for the change in the bond rate.

Beaudry and Koop's (1993) CDR model is designed to capture the asymmetric dynamic caused by the fact that negative shocks to real and financial variables tend to have temporary effects but positive shocks tend to have permanent effects. This asymmetry is embodied in the model through the inclusion of a CDR term, which measures the distance from the previous peak of the variable to the current value. This term is positive when the current value is below the previous peak:

$$(5.8) \quad CDR_t = max(Y_{t-j})_{j \geq 0} - Y_t .$$

Inclusion of this CDR term converts an otherwise linear model (like an AR model) into a nonlinear model:

Figure 5.6 DLIP Models: Transition Functions TAR and STAR

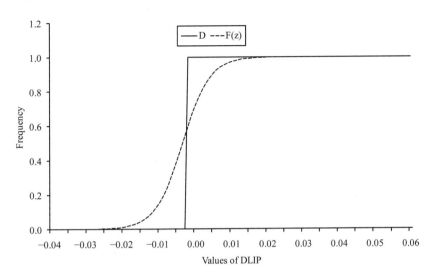

SOURCE: Authors' calculations.

(5.9) $\Theta(L)_t \Delta Y_t = \delta + [\Omega(L) - 1]CDR_t + \varepsilon_t$.

Here $\Theta(L)$ and $\Omega(L)$ represent polynomials in the lag operator L, a convenient way to represent that there are lags of ΔY and lags of CDR in the equation. If the coefficient on the CDR term is positive, then ΔY grows faster when CDR increases—that is, when the recession is deeper. In other words, ΔY grows fasters after a negative shock has placed the economy in a deep recession. When the economy recovers and is growing above its previous peak, this extra growth in ΔY is eliminated. In this case, positive shocks will have longer-lasting positive effects on ΔY than negative shocks. Of course, if the coefficient on the CDR term is < 0, the opposite case holds: a negative shock leads to more persistent performance below the previous peak.

To allow for possible nonlinear effects from the financial markets and the real sector, we investigate two versions of a CDR-type model, one for industrial production and one for stock prices. The CDR term has a positive value when industrial production is below its previous peak, and the CDB term has a positive value when the S&P 500 is below its

Table 5.8 LSTAR for DINT, January 1955–December 2004

Constant	1.95E-06	(8.07E-06);	$p = 0.8090$
DINT(−1)	—	—	—
DINT(−2)	—	—	—
ER(−1)	−0.0118	(0.0028);	$p = 0.0000$
ER(−2)	0.0083	(0.0017);	$p = 0.000$
DINT(−1) × F	0.3995	(0.0461);	$p = 0.0000$
DINT(−2) × F	−0.2235	(0.0409);	$p = 0.0000$
ER(−1) × F	0.0129	(0.0029);	$p = 0.0000$
ER(−2) × F	−0.0078	(0.0170);	$p = 0.0000$
Gamma	464.68	(183.01);	$p = 0.0014$
Threshold for DINT(−1)	−4.81E-04	(4.78E-05);	$p = 0.0000$
R^2		0.2276	
Std. error		1.94E-04	
SIC		−14.1756	
Log likelihood		4,281.459	

NOTE: — = data not available.
SOURCE: Authors' calculations.

Table 5.9 TAR for DINT, January 1955–December 2004

Constant	1.29E-06	(7.97E-06);	$p = 0.8710$
DINT(−1)	—	—	—
DINT(−2)	—	—	—
ER(−1)	−0.0099	(0.0014);	$p = 0.0000$
ER(−2)	0.0086	(0.0014);	$p = 0.0000$
DINT(−1) × δ	0.3869	(0.0439);	$p = 0.0000$
DINT(−2) × δ	−0.2159	(0.0401);	$p = 0.0000$
ER(−1) × δ	0.0108	(0.0014);	$p = 0.0000$
ER(−2) × δ	−0.0080	(0.0014);	$p = 0.0000$
Threshold for DINT(−1)		−0.00048	
R^2		0.2245	
Std. error		1.94E-04	
SIC		−14.1928	
Log likelihood		4,280.239	

NOTE: — = data not available.
SOURCE: Authors' calculations.

Figure 5.7 Histogram for Changes in the Interest Rate

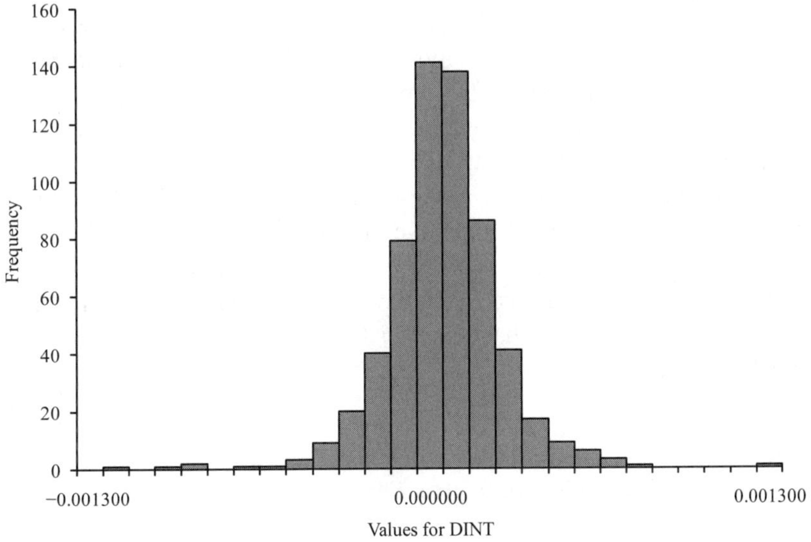

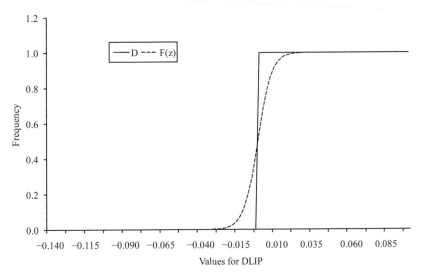

SOURCE: Authors' calculations.

Figure 5.8 DINT Models: Transition Functions TAR and STAR

SOURCE: Authors' calculations.

previous peak. The two graphs in Figure 5.9 display the values for CDR and CDB and illustrate the differences in their time series histories.

To investigate this specification of nonlinearity, we took the linear models presented in Table 5.3 and augmented them with both terms—CDR and CDB. Neither the CDR term nor the CDB term was significant for the change in the bond interest rate, indicating that the CDR class of models was not appropriate for that variable. In contrast, both the CDR and the CDB terms were significant in the model for the change in the log of industrial production (see Table 5.10). The sum of the coefficients on the CDR term is positive, meaning that industrial production grows faster after a negative shock to industrial production. This means that negative real shocks have shorter lasting effects than positive real shocks and industrial production tends to grow relatively rapidly after

Figure 5.9 Current Depth of Recession and Current Depth of Stocks, January 1955–December 2004

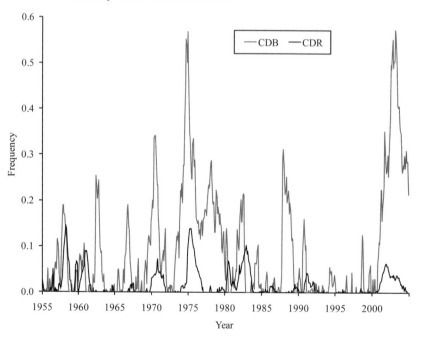

NOTE: CDR stands for current depth of recession. CDB stands for current depth of stocks.
SOURCE: Authors' calculations.

Table 5.10 CDR Model for DLIP

Constant	0.0023 (0.0006);	$p = 0.0001$
DLIP(−1)	0.1296 (0.0872);	$p = 0.1378$
DLIP(−2)	0.1229 (0.0411);	$p = 0.0029$
ER(−1)	0.0770 (0.0258);	$p = 0.0030$
ER(−2)	—	—
DINT(−1)	4.9270 (1.5277);	$p = 0.0013$
CDR(−1)	−0.1840 (0.0997);	$p = 0.0655$
CDR(−2)	0.2241 (0.0958);	$p = 0.0197$
CDB(−1)	0.0611 (0.0286);	$p = 0.0335$
CDB(−2)	−0.0722 (0.0278);	$p = 0.0096$
R^2	0.2274	
Std. error	0.0079	
SIC	−6.7599	
Log likelihood	2,056.741	

NOTE: — = data not available.
SOURCE: Authors' calculations.

recessions. In contrast, the sign of the sum of the coefficients on the CDB term is negative. This suggests that industrial production grows more slowly after stock market declines.

Only the CDR term was significant in the excess returns equation, and the estimated model is presented in Table 5.11. The coefficient on the CDR term is positive, suggesting that excess returns grow faster

Table 5.11 CDR Model for ER

Constant	1.19E-03 (1.59E-03);	$p = 0.4529$
ER(−1)	0.1996 (0.0399);	$p = 0.0000$
DINT(−1)	−26.4039 (6.2711);	$p = 0.0000$
CDR(−1)	0.0960 (0.0486);	$p = 0.0486$
R^2	0.0902	
Std. error	0.0331	
SIC	−3.9400	

SOURCE: Authors' calculations.

when industrial production is in its "recovery" phase and expanding out of a recession.

FORECAST EVALUATION

The above models were all estimated over a sample period from January of 1955 to December of 2004 (1955.01–2004.12). We reserved the final 58 data points, 2005.01–2009.10, for an out-of-sample forecasting comparison. The idea is to estimate the model up to 2004.12, as if we are actually in 2004.12, and use that information and parameter estimates to forecast in 2005.01. Then we update the sample to 1955.01–2005.01 and use that information to forecast 2005.2. We continue this exercise through our last data point, forecasting 2009.10 using the sample 1955.01–2009.09. In this way our forecasts are all constructed using only information available at the time of the forecast.

The above description is an ideal, however, as data revisions occur after the fact, and we have used data available to us late in 2009. If data revisions occurred—and they certainly did to industrial production—then our entire sample in 2009 contains data different from what a forecaster would have available in real time. This is a topic of great interest in the current literature but not one we deal with in this study. Fortunately, financial series such as stock prices and returns are not typically subject to the data revision problem.

An important issue is how to judge forecasting performance. We can calculate how far off each individual forecast is for the various models, and average the forecast errors over our 58-data-point forecasting sample. More often, we calculate the average of the squared forecast errors, and still more often we calculate the square root of the average of the squared forecast errors, or the root mean square forecasting error (RMSFE). This is probably the most widely cited measure of forecast accuracy. Another widely used measure is the average of the absolute value of the forecasting errors, the mean absolute forecasting error (MAFE). Other loss functions are possible, including measures of turning points and loss functions based on utility or profit functions, but we will not pursue those alternatives here.

Table 5.12 provides the out-of-sample measures of the RMSFE and MAFE for our three variables (DINT, DLIP, ER) and our four models (linear, TAR, STAR, CDR). For excess returns we also provide a random walk model. We highlight the model that achieves the best (lowest) value for each variable. For the RMSFE criterion, the best DINT model is the linear model. The TAR model does a particularly poor job. For DLIP, the best RMSFE values are given by the STAR model, followed by the TAR model. The linear model only does better than the CDR model. Finally, for ER the best RMSFE value is provided by the CDR model, and both models beat a random walk.

For the MAFE criterion, we again find that the best forecasts of DINT are provided by the linear model, although here the STAR model appears to do almost as well as the linear model. For DLIP, the best forecasts are from the TAR model, followed by the STAR model, with the linear model third. Again the CDR model does the worst of the four. For ER, the best forecasts come from the CDR model, followed by the linear model, with the random walk bringing up the rear.

More insight into the relative forecast performance can be gleaned from examining the forecasts and forecast errors. Figure 5.10 plots the values for the changes in the bond rate, DINT, along with forecasts of DINT from the linear model and the TAR model. These are graphed on the left-hand scale. The actual values are represented by the line identi-

Table 5.12 Performance Measures for Out-of-Sample Forecasts, January 2005–October 2009

RMSE loss criterion	Linear	TAR	STAR	CDR	Random walk
DINT	1.76E-04	3.40E-04	1.92E-04		—
DLIP	8.28E-03	7.64E-03	7.54E-03	8.64E-03	—
ER	4.52E-02	—	—	4.46E-02	4.77E-02

MAE loss criterion	Linear	TAR	STAR	CDR	Random walk
DINT	1.33E-04	1.82E-04	1.35E-04		—
DLIP	5.67E-03	5.16E-03	5.28E-03	5.72E-03	—
ER	2.90E-02	—	—	2.84E-02	3.11E-02

NOTE: — = model not estimated; blank = not applicable.
SOURCE: Authors' calculations.

**Figure 5.10 Changes in the Bond Rate and Forecasts, January 2005–
September 2009**

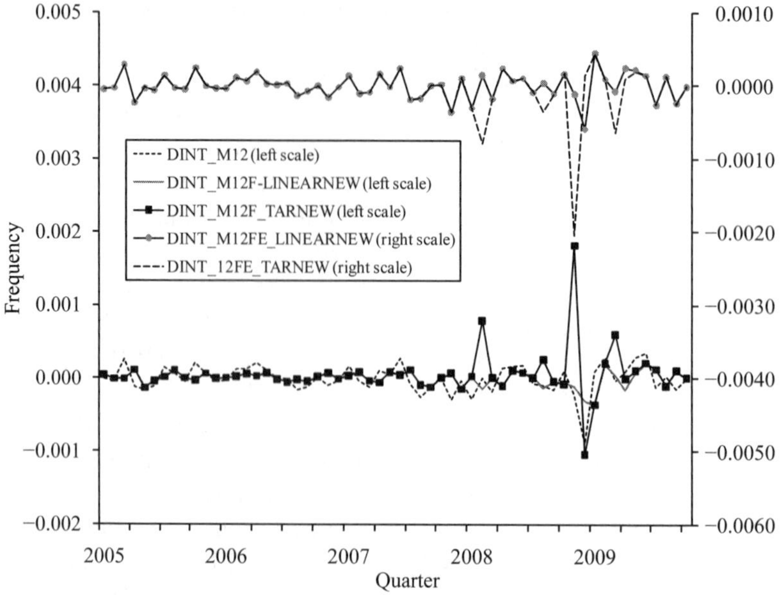

SOURCE: Authors' calculations.

fied in the legend as "DINT_M12," and the forecasts are the other lines.
There is a big difference between the actual values and the forecast
from the TAR model in the middle of 2008. The TAR model predicted a
large value for DINT at this time, but the large value failed to material-
ize. The difference between the actual value of DINT and the forecast
from the TAR model is about −0.002, a large value that led the TAR
model to perform quite poorly based on the RMSFE. The forecast errors themselves are plotted at the top, and on the right-hand scale, of
Figure 5.10. The large downward spike in mid-2008 is the TAR model
forecast error we have just discussed.

Figure 5.11 plots the forecasts, actual value, and forecast errors for
changes in the log of industrial production. The line with black squares
in the lower part of the graph is the actual value of DLIP, which experienced large upward and downward moves in the latter half of 2008.
These movements in DLIP were not forecast by either the linear or TAR

Figure 5.11   Forecasts, Actual Value, and Forecast Errors for Changes in the Log of Industrial Production, January 1955–September 2009

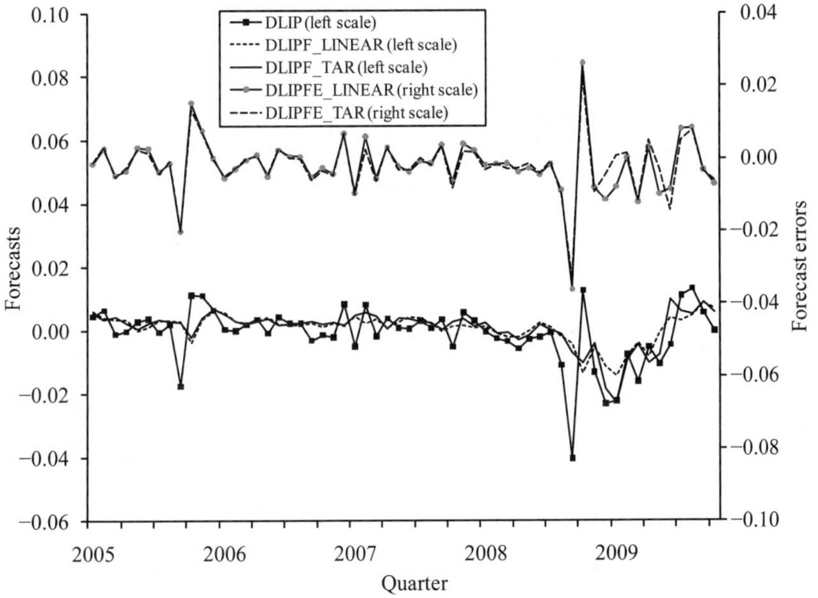

SOURCE: Authors' calculations.

models. Hence this movement generated forecast errors, which can be seen in the top of Figure 5.11 on lines graphed against the right-hand scale. The forecast errors from the linear and TAR models seem similar in Figure 5.11, although there is some discrepancy near the end of 2008 and at the beginning of 2009. During this period the TAR model does slightly better, and this leads to the TAR model having a lower RMSFE in Table 5.12.

Finally, Figure 5.12 plots linear and CDR forecasts of excess returns. Again we see there was a large downward spike in ER in the fourth quarter of 2008 that was not forecast by either the linear or the CDR models. Thus this spike shows up in the top of Figure 5.12 as forecast errors for both the linear and CDR models. As with industrial production in Figure 5.11, it is difficult to see much difference in the forecasts, or forecast errors, from the linear and CDR models. The main

Figure 5.12 Linear and CDR Forecasts of Excess Returns, January 1955–September 2009

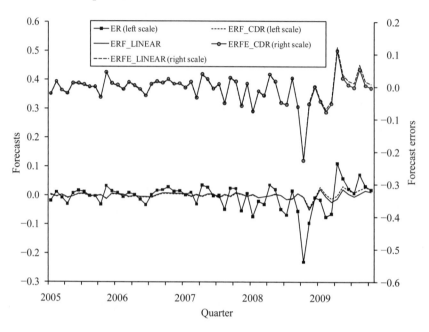

SOURCE: Authors' calculations.

difference appears beginning in the middle of 2009, and this small difference leads to the CDR model having somewhat lower RMSFE values compared to the linear model.

One issue with results such as in Table 5.12 is the lack of a measure for saying just how much better one model's forecasts are over another's. We would like a way of answering this question. Usually this is phrased as an issue of statistical significance. We want to know whether, for the ER model, the CDR model forecasts are statistically significantly better than the forecasts of the linear model.

There are a variety of tests available for answering this question. A classic test of forecast accuracy is the Diebold and Mariano (1995) test, which has as its null hypothesis that two forecasts are equally accurate by the chosen criterion (say RMSFE), and the alternative that one of the two is better. Another test is called the encompassing test, which compares two forecasts and asks whether, given one forecast, there is additional useful information in the second forecast. If the answer is yes, then you might want to combine the two forecasts. If the answer is no, then you might want to use the best forecast and ignore the second forecast as containing no additional information once you have the first forecast. Encompassing tests have been in use for quite some time, and some early advocates include Chong and Hendry (1986) and Harvey, Leybourne, and Newbold (1989).

In conducting these tests, an important practical issue is whether or not your forecasting models are nested. The initial Diebold and Mariano test was designed for use with nonnested forecasting models, which are basically two unrelated forecasting models. Nested forecasting models, in contrast, are models where one model is a subset of another model. In our models, the linear model is nested inside the CDR model. If we just eliminate the CDR terms—say, by setting the coefficients on the CDR terms to zero—we get back the linear model. Similarly, our TAR and STAR models also nest the linear model. If we just set the terms multiplying the transition variable all to zero, then we have a one-regime linear model.

Statistical comparisons of nested models bring up complications relative to comparisons of nonnested models. This issue has been explored by a number of authors, including work by West (1996), Clark (1999), McCracken (2000), and Clark and McCracken (2001), and we refer the interested reader to those papers.

Giacomini and White (2006) suggest a new approach to statistical comparisons of forecasts from nested models. Basically they have a version of the Diebold and Mariano test that works for nested models, a model based on the idea of conditional forecast comparisons, and we use their approach here. In Table 5.13 we report tests of the RMSFE loss function for our various models. In these tests we select a baseline model and compare our other models to the baseline. For the DINT and DLIP forecasts we use the linear model as the baseline. For the ER forecasts we use the random walk model as the baseline.

For the DINT forecasts we see in Table 5.12 that the smallest RMSFE was for the linear model. Thus the test results in Table 5.13 are basically tests of whether the baseline linear model is statistically significantly better than the TAR or STAR models. The answer is that while the linear model has a lower RMSFE, it is not statistically sig-

Table 5.13 GW Version of DM Test (unconditional)—RMSE Loss Function

Variable to forecast	Random walk	Linear	TAR	STAR	CDR/CDB
DINT	—	Baseline	1.2871	0.9974	—
			($p = 0.203$)	($p = 0.323$)	
DLIP	—	Baseline	1.5092	1.2880	−0.7353
			($p = 0.131$)	($p = 0.198$)	($p = 0.465$)
ER	Baseline	1.5329			0.5257
		($p = 0.125$)			($p = 0.601$)

NOTE: — = model not estimated; blank = not applicable.
SOURCE: Authors' calculations.

nificantly lower than either of the two nonlinear models. This is even true for the TAR model, which appeared to perform quite poorly in terms of RMSFE. Still, this is no victory for the nonlinear models. A linear model is much easier to estimate and to use for forecasting. If a linear model gives forecasts that are as good or better than the nonlinear model alternatives, then we would usually avoid going to the trouble of forecasting from a nonlinear model.

For the DLIP forecasts, we see in Table 5.12 that the lowest RMSFE values were generated by the two nonlinear models. In Table 5.13 we see that even though TAR and STAR both provided better RMSFE values, the improvement was not statistically significant. The TAR model has the best marginal probability value, 13.1 percent, but that means that at conventional significance levels of 5 or even 10 percent we would not reject the hypothesis of equal RMSFE for the linear and TAR forecasts.

For the ER forecasts, we compared both the linear model and the CDR model to a random walk baseline. In Table 5.12 we see that the linear model had better RMSFE values than the random walk model, and that the CDR model had better RMSFE values than the linear model, but in Table 5.13 we see that neither the linear nor the CDR model improves on the random walk model in a statistically significant amount.

The results for the DLIP and ER forecasts are disappointing for fans of the nonlinear model. In both cases a nonlinear model or models made improvements in terms of RMSFE values, but these improvements were not statistically significant.

In Table 5.14 we report a similar exercise using the MAFE criterion. Here we find a bit better news for the nonlinear models. For DINT we again find that the linear model is best, but for DLIP we find that the forecasts from the TAR model are statistically significantly better than forecasts from the linear model. The marginal probability value is 3.2 percent, indicating that at standard significance levels of 5 percent we would reject the hypothesis of equal forecasting accuracy—in terms of MAFE—of the linear model and the TAR model.

For the ER model the results in Table 5.14 indicate that forecasts from the linear model are statistically significantly better than forecasts from the random walk model. But we find the disappointing result that forecasts from the CDR model are statistically insignificantly different in accuracy from forecasts of the random walk model. Even though the CDR model generated a better MAFE value compared to the linear model, the variability of the forecasts from the CDR model means that the difference is judged to be statistically insignificant.

Overall, then, our forecast evaluation indicates only weak support for the superiority of forecasts of DLIP from a TAR model, and even weaker support for using a CDR model to forecast ER. We find no support for using anything other than a linear model for forecasting DINT. Basically we find the result, familiar to many in this literature, that nonlinear models appear to fit well in estimation samples but that these models don't fair nearly as well in out-of-sample forecasting exercises.

Table 5.14 GW Version of DM Test (unconditional)—MAE Loss Function

	Random walk	Linear	TAR	STAR	CDR/CDB
DINT	—	Baseline	1.3157 $(p = 0.194)$	1.6432 $(p = 0.106)$	—
DLIP	—	Baseline	2.1438 $(p = 0.032)$	1.4329 $(p = 0.152)$	−0.2010 $(p = 0.841)$
ER	Baseline	2.0097 $(p = 0.044)$			0.7158 $(p = 0.477)$

NOTE: — = model not estimated; blank = not applicable.
SOURCE: Authors' calculations.

SOME COMMENTS ON MULTIPLE-STEP-AHEAD
FORECASTING

In the analysis above we have investigated the ability of a set of
nonlinear models to generate forecasts of two financial variables and
industrial production that are better than forecasts from a linear model.
This analysis has looked at one-step-ahead forecasts, or forecasts made
at time t for the value of variables at time $t + 1$. It is also possible, of
course, to construct multiple-step-ahead forecasts—forecasts made at
time t for the value of variables at time $t + 2$ or later (better represented
as $t + H$, where H stands for the horizon) and for multiple-step-ahead
forecasts $H > 1$.

Nonlinear models present particular challenges when constructing multiple-step-ahead forecasts. For linear models the law of iterated
expectations and the use of the linear expectation operator on linear
equations makes multiple-step-ahead forecasting a straightforward
extension of one-step-ahead forecasts. To see this, consider a simple
AR(1) model:

$$(5.10) \quad y_t = \beta y_{t-1} + \varepsilon_t .$$

To calculate the one-step-ahead forecast we rewrite Equation (5.10) for
time $t + 1$ and take expectations conditioned on knowledge of the value
of y at time t:

$$(5.11) \quad y_{t+1} = \beta y_t + \varepsilon_{t+1} .$$

Then, taking expectations conditioned on knowledge of y_t, we have

$$(5.12) \quad E(y_{t+1} | y_t) = \beta y_t .$$

To think about a two-step-ahead forecast made at time t, rewrite Equation 5.10 for time $t + 2$ and iteratively substitute to write the result as a
function of the value of y at time t:

$$(5.13) \quad y_{t+2} = \beta y_{t+1} + \varepsilon_{t+2} = \beta(\beta y_t + \varepsilon_{t+1}) + \varepsilon_{t+2} = \beta^2 y_t + \beta \varepsilon_{t+1} + \varepsilon_{t+2} .$$

Then, taking expectations conditioned on knowledge of y_t, we have

(5.14) $E(y_{t+2}|y_t) = \beta^2 y_t$.

Thus the two-step-ahead forecast in Equation 5.14 is a simple extension of the one-step-ahead forecast in Equation 5.12. While the above is a particularly simple model in terms of notation, the principle holds more generally in forecasts from linear models.

Consider now a nonlinear model. A simple TAR model would be

(5.15) $y_t = \beta y_{t-1} + \gamma y_{t-1} \times I(y_{t-1} < c) + \varepsilon_t$.

To calculate the one-step-ahead forecast, we rewrite Equation (5.15) for time $t + 1$ as

(5.16) $y_{t+1} = \beta y_t + \gamma y_t \times I(y_t < c) + \varepsilon_{t+1}$.

Then, taking expectations conditioned on knowledge of y_t, we have

(5.17) $E(y_{t+1}|y_t) = \beta y_t + \gamma y_t \times I(y_t < c)$.

So far this looks straightforward, much like the one-step-ahead forecast from the linear model. However, consider the two-step-ahead forecast made at time t. Rewrite Equation (5.15) for time $t + 2$ and iteratively substitute to write the result as a function of the value of y at time t :

(5.18) $y_{t+2} = \beta y_{t+1} + \gamma y_{t+1} \times I(y_{t+1} < c) + \varepsilon_{t+2}$

or

$$y_{t+2} = \beta[\beta y_t + \gamma y_t \times I(y_t < c) + \varepsilon_{t+1}] + \gamma[\beta y_t + \gamma y_t \times$$

$$I(y_t < c) + \varepsilon_{t+1}] \times I\{[\beta y_t + \gamma y_t \times I(y_t < c) + \varepsilon_{t+1}] < c\} + \varepsilon_{t+2}$$.

Then, taking expectations conditioned on knowledge of y_t, we have

$$(5.19) \quad E(y_{t+2}|y_t) = \beta[\beta y_t + \gamma y_t \times I(y_t < c)] + \gamma[\beta y_t + \gamma y_t \times I(y_t < c)]$$

$$\times E\left(I\{[\beta y_t + \gamma y_t \times I(y_t < c) + \varepsilon_{t+1}] < c\}|y_t\right) + E\{\varepsilon_{t+1}$$

$$\times I[\varepsilon_{t+1} < c - \beta y_t - \gamma y_t \times I(y_t < c)]|y_t\}.$$

Clearly, Equation (5.19) is not a straightforward extension of Equation (5.17). In fact, the last term in Equation (5.17) involves expectation of the disturbance term ε_{t+1} interacted with a function of the same disturbance term ε_{t+1}. It is evident, then, that the two-step-ahead forecast involves considerations of higher moments than the mean. To put this in practice requires distributional assumptions on the error term or else some sort of bootstrap procedure to calculate expectations from the empirically realized (i.e., estimated) disturbances. None of this makes multiple-step-ahead forecasts from nonlinear models impossible, but they are much more involved than such forecasts in a linear model, and as this chapter is already quite long we do not pursue such forecasts here.

CONCLUSION

Our study demonstrates once again how nonlinear models can fit very well in-sample and yet struggle to outperform linear models in out-of-sample forecasting. This finding is not unusual, but it is frustrating to proponents of nonlinear modeling. Nonlinear modelers usually exert care in trying to avoid overfitting within sample, and yet the out-of-sample performance difficulties point to overfitting as one possible source of the problem. The exact reason for these difficulties with forecasts from nonlinear models remains an open issue.

References

Beaudry, Paul, and Gary Koop. 1993. "Do Recessions Permanently Change Output?" *Journal of Monetary Economics* 31(2): 149–163.

Bradley, Michael D., and Dennis W. Jansen. 1997. "Nonlinear Business Cycle Dynamics: Cross-Country Evidence on the Persistence of Aggregate Shocks." *Economic Inquiry* 35(3): 495–509.

———. 2000. "Are Business Cycle Dynamics the Same across Countries? Testing Linearity around the Globe." *Studies in Nonlinear Dynamics and Econometrics* 4(2): 51–71.

———. 2004. "Forecasting with a Nonlinear Dynamic Model of Stock Returns and Industrial Production." *International Journal of Forecasting* 20(2): 321–342.

Chan, Kung-sik, and Howell Tong. 1986. "On Estimating Thresholds in Autoregressive Models." *Journal of Time Series Analysis* 7(3): 179–190.

Cheng, Bing, and D.M. Titterington. 1994. "Neural Networks: A Review from a Statistical Perspective." *Statistical Science* 9(1): 2–30.

Chong, Yock Y., and David F. Hendry. 1986. "Econometric Evaluation of Linear Macro-Economic Models." *Review of Economic Studies* 53(4): 671–690.

Clark, Todd E. 1999. "Finite-Sample Properties of Tests for Equal Forecast Accuracy." *Journal of Forecasting* 18(7): 489–504.

Clark, Todd E., and Michael W. McCracken. 2001. "Tests of Equal Forecast Accuracy and Encompassing for Nested Models." *Journal of Econometrics* 105(1): 85–110.

Diebold, Francis X., and Roberto S. Mariano. 1995. "Comparing Predictive Accuracy." *Journal of Business and Economic Statistics* 13(3): 253–263.

Falk, Barry. 1986. "Further Evidence on the Asymmetric Behavior of Economic Time Series over the Business Cycle." *Journal of Political Economy* 94(5): 1096–1109.

Giacomini, Raffaella, and Halbert White. 2006. "Tests of Conditional Predictive Ability." *Econometrica* 74(6): 1545–1578.

Granger, Clive W.J., and Timo Teräsvirta. 1993. *Modelling Dynamic Nonlinear Relationships*. Oxford: Oxford University Press.

Granger, Clive W.J., Timo Teräsvirta, and Heather M. Anderson. 1993. "Modeling Nonlinearity over the Business Cycle." In *New Research on Business Cycles, Indicators, and Forecasting*, James H. Stock and Mark W. Watson, eds. Chicago: University of Chicago Press, pp. 311–326.

Hamilton, James D. 1989. "A New Approach to the Economic Analysis of Nonstationary Time Series and the Business Cycle." *Econometrica* 57(2): 357–384.

Hansen, Bruce E. 1997. "Inference in TAR Models." *Studies in Nonlinear Dynamics and Econometrics* 2(1): 1–14.

Harvey, David I., Stephen J. Leybourne, and Paul Newbold. 1989. "Tests for Forecast Encompassing." *Journal of Business and Economic Statistics* 16(2): 254–259.

Jansen, Dennis W., and Wankeun Oh. 1999. "Modeling Nonlinearity of Business Cycles: Choosing between the CDR and STAR Models." *Review of Economics and Statistics* 81(2): 344–349.

Li, Qi, and Jeffrey Scott Racine. 2007. *Nonparametric Econometrics: Theory and Practice*. Princeton, NJ: Princeton University Press.

Luukkonen, Ritva, Pentti Saikkonen, and Timo Teräsvirta. 1988. "Testing Linearity against Smooth Transition Autoregressive Models." *Biometrika* 75(3): 491–499.

McCracken, Michael W. 2000. "Robust Out-of-Sample Inference." *Journal of Econometrics* 99(2): 195–223.

Neftçi, Salih N. 1984. "Are Economic Time Series Asymmetric over the Business Cycle?" *Journal of Political Economy* 92(2): 307–328.

Pesaran, M. Hashem, and Simon M. Potter. 1997. "A Floor and Ceiling Model of U.S. Output." *Journal of Economic Dynamics and Control* 21(4–5): 661–696.

Potter, Simon M. 1995. "A Nonlinear Approach to U.S. GNP." *Journal of Applied Econometrics* 10(2): 109–125.

Shiller, Robert S. 2011. *Online Data*. Hew Haven, CT: Yale University, Department of Economics. http://www.econ.yale.edu/~shiller/data.htm (accessed April 6, 2011).

Teräsvirta, Timo. 1994. "Specification, Estimation, and Evaluation of Smooth Transition Autoregressive Models." *Journal of the American Statistical Association* 89(425): 208–218.

Teräsvirta, Timo, and Heather M. Anderson. 1992. "Characterizing Nonlinearities in Business Cycles Using Smooth Transition Autoregressive Models." *Journal of Applied Econometrics* 7(S1): S119–S136.

Tong, Howell. 1990. *Non-Linear Time Series: A Dynamical System Approach*. Oxford: Oxford University Press.

Tsay, Ruey S. 1989. "Testing and Modeling Threshold Autoregressive Processes." *Journal of the American Statistical Association* 84(405): 231–240.

van Dijk, Dick, and Philip Hans Franses. 1999. "Modeling Multiple Regimes in the Business Cycle." *Macroeconomic Dynamics* 3(3): 311–340.

West, Kenneth D. 1996. "Asymptotic Inference about Predictive Ability." *Econometrica* 64(5): 1067–1084.

6

Perspectives on Evaluating Macroeconomic Forecasts

H.O. Stekler

George Washington University

Over the past 50 or so years, I have been concerned with the quality of economic forecasts and have written both about the procedures for evaluating these predictions and the results that were obtained from these evaluations. In this chapter I provide some perspectives on the issues involved in judging the quality of these forecasts. These include the reasons for evaluating forecasts, the questions that have been asked in these evaluations, the statistical tools that have been used, and the generally accepted results. (I do also present some new material that has not yet been published.) I do this in two parts: first focusing on short-run gross domestic product (GDP) and inflation predictions and then turning to labor market forecasts.

The process of forecasting involves a number of sequential steps. Part of that process is concerned with evaluating either the forecasts themselves or the methods that generated the predictions. This evaluation may occur either when past forecasts are examined prior to preparing the next one or in a postmortem session to determine what went wrong and what can be learned from the errors. However, there are different perspectives or approaches for conducting these examinations. These differences may occur because some forecasts are model-based while others are derived primarily from the judgmental approach. There is a second issue. Originally, the evaluations were concerned with judging a particular model or individual. A more recent development has been to determine the value that the forecast has for the users of that prediction.

The original approach calculated a variety of statistics that measured the errors of the forecasts and then compared these errors with those generated by alternative methods or individuals. The newer approach for forecast evaluation is to base it on the loss functions of the users (Pesaran and Skouras 2002). Elliott and Timmermann (2008), in summarizing the theoretical literature on how to evaluate forecasts, take the same approach. These studies definitely suggest that the preferred evaluation methodology utilize decision-based methods; Pesaran and Skouras, however, note that it has had limited use, and that most studies have focused on statistical measures to evaluate the skills of the forecaster or the accuracy of the model.[1] There are many reasons why the decision-based methods have not been used, including technical difficulties and the huge amount of data required to describe the decision environment, particularly the loss functions of the users.

The theoretical procedures provide the guidelines for undertaking forecast evaluations, but since there are problems in applying them, they have not yet yielded much information about the quality of the forecasts or an understanding of the types of errors that occur or their causes. Even though we cannot, in general, evaluate the cost of the forecast errors in the context of decision functions, I will present one particular result where it was possible to use this approach.[2]

Statistical measures have been the most common method for evaluating forecasts, and they have provided many insights about the quality of the forecasts and their limitations. I will, therefore, focus on that approach. These measures also provide us with the ability to obtain information about the forecasting process and why particular errors occurred.

This chapter proceeds as follows. I first present a list of questions that should be addressed in any evaluation of macroeconomic forecasts; this list was taken from an old paper of mine (Stekler 1991a). That paper also presented the statistical methods that could be used to address those questions. In the intervening 20 years, forecasters have both developed new techniques for answering the original questions and asked additional questions. I will discuss these in the context of the original questions.

Our macroeconomic forecast evaluations have primarily been concerned with the predictions of GDP growth and inflation. I will, therefore, summarize some of the findings relating to these two variables. In making macro forecasts, economists also estimate the unemployment rate, but these forecasts have not been analyzed as extensively. Consequently, there is a limited amount of information about the quality of these forecasts.

Moreover, in analyzing labor markets in a macroeconomic growth context, long-term projections of annual employment by industry and occupation are sometimes also issued. Not as much attention has been paid to the procedures for evaluating these projections. I will present some findings about these forecasts, utilizing a statistic that has not conventionally been used in evaluations. There are also many types of regional forecasts, but I will only discuss the population projections of the Census Bureau. I conclude with a summary of the findings and suggest topics that warrant further research.

QUESTIONS ADDRESSED IN MACROECONOMIC FORECAST EVALUATIONS

In 1991, I asked a number of questions, some of which are related, that can be and have been used in forecast evaluations (Stekler 1991a). These questions are all statistical in nature and describe the characteristics of the forecasting method or the particular forecaster. The main questions are

- How good is Method A (Forecaster X)?
- Do the forecasts show systematic errors?
- Are all methods (forecasters) equally good?
- Is Method A (Forecaster X) significantly better than Method B (Forecaster Y)?
- Does Forecast M contain information not in Forecast N?
- Does Forecaster X produce forecasts that are useful to users?

How Good is Method A (Forecaster X)?

If the forecasts are quantitative, the first question is answered by using some error metric, usually mean square error or mean square percentage error, and comparing it with the similar error metric of a benchmark or naive model.[3] On the other hand, different procedures are used to assess nonquantitative macroeconomic forecasting techniques, which are primarily concerned with predicting whether a cyclical turn will occur. These forecasting methods are based on indicators. Originally, rules were used for determining whether an indicator was signaling a turn. (See Stekler 1991b.) More recently, models that predict the probability of a cyclical turn have been developed, and probability scoring rules such as the Brier Score have been used to evaluate these forecasts. Further analysis of these qualitative forecasts is beyond the scope of this paper.

Bias and Efficiency

Accurate forecasts should be unbiased (not have systematic errors) and should use all available information. Bias and efficiency tests are used to determine whether there are systematic errors. These tests are usually derived from the Mincer-Zarnowitz equation:

(6.1a) $A_t = \alpha + \beta F_t + e_t$, where

A_t and F_t refer to the actual and forecast values (Mincer and Zarnowitz 1969). The condition for unbiasedness and weak form efficiency is that $\alpha = 0$ and $\beta = 1$. An alternative test for bias is

(6.1b) $A_t - \beta F_t = c + e_t$,

with the null that $c = 0$ (Holden and Peel 1990). These tests are applied to one individual's forecasts at one horizon.

A newer and more sophisticated methodology has been developed by Davies and Lahiri (1995, 1999) and has been applied to surveys that contain the forecasts of many individuals or organizations, e.g., the Survey of Professional Forecasters (SPF) or Blue Chip Forecasters. The use of this methodology permits an analysis of multidimensional forecasts, i.e., many forecasters each making a prediction for a target year at several horizons.[4] The errors can be decomposed as

(6.2a) $A_t - F_{ith} = \Phi_i + \lambda_{th} + e_{ith}$

and

(6.2b) $\lambda_{th} = \sum u_{tj}$, where

F_{ith} is the forecast made by the ith forecaster for year t at an h month horizon, Φ_i represents the specific bias of each individual, and λ_{th} represents the shocks that were not anticipated. This model can identify the specific sources of each forecaster's errors.

Using the Davies-Lahiri methodology it is no longer necessary to confine the evaluation of the predictions obtained from a survey to the "consensus" forecast. It has the inherent advantage that the opposing biases of individuals can make the mean (median) forecast look unbiased even when, in fact, the individual forecasts from which the mean is calculated are all biased.

Comparing Forecasters and Benchmarks

Nonparametric procedures have been used to determine whether all forecasters are equally accurate. For each set of forecasts, the errors of each forecaster are ranked according to their accuracy. If the accuracy of all forecasters were equal, their rankings would have the same expected values. It is thus possible to test the hypothesis that all forecasters have equal rankings (and are equally good). The chi-square goodness-of-fit test statistic, x^2, is used. (See Batchelor 1990.)

The fourth question asks whether a particular method (forecaster) is significantly more accurate than another method (forecaster). Originally, Theil's U coefficient was the basis of comparison:

$$(6.3) \quad U = \sqrt{(e_{f,t})^2} / \sqrt{(e_{n,t})^2} \ ,$$

where $(e_{f,t})$ is the error of the forecast that is being evaluated and $(e_{n,t})$ is the error of the naive benchmark. This naive model can be either a no-change or the same change as the last period prediction. At a minimum, the forecasts should be more accurate than naive models and U must be less than 1. Statistical models, such as ARIMA, have also been used as benchmarks, and new statistics for comparing models have been developed.

Currently the Diebold-Mariano (DM) statistic is the preferred methodology for testing whether there is a statistically significant difference in accuracy between any two sets of forecasts (Diebold and Mariano 1995). That statistic (Equation 6.4) has been modified by Harvey, Leybourne, and Newbold (1997), and their modification has resulted in an improvement in the behavior of the test statistic for moderately sized samples:

$$(6.4) \quad S_1^* = S_1\left(\frac{T+1-2(h+1)+h(h+1)/T}{T}\right)^{-1/2}, \quad S_1 = \frac{\overline{d}}{[\hat{V}(\overline{d})]^{1/2}},$$

where h is the horizon, $\overline{d}$ is the mean absolute difference of the prediction errors, $\hat{V}(\overline{d})$ is the estimated variance, S_1 is the original DM statistic, and S_1^* is the modified DM statistic. The modified DM test statistic is estimated with Newey-West corrected standard errors that allow for heteroskedastic autocorrelated errors (Newey and West 1987).

Several procedures have been developed to determine whether one forecast contains information not embodied in another procedure. One involves combining the two sets of forecasts. If the variance of the combined forecasts is not significantly less than the variance of the prediction that is being analyzed, then this particular forecast does not contain additional useful information. This analysis is similar to the concept of encompassing, where a model that encompasses another contains the information of the latter.

Directional Accuracy: A New Approach

Even though the analysis does not directly use utility functions, the final question listed above relates to the usefulness of a forecast to a decision maker. It concerns the directional accuracy of the forecast. Merton (1981), in analyzing financial forecasts, indicates that they have value if the signs of the predicted and actual changes are similar. The various tests that have been implemented seek to determine whether the sign of the forecast change is probabilistically independent of the actual change. If the hypothesis that the forecasts are independent of the observed events is rejected, then the forecasts can be said to have value.

Schnader and Stekler (1990) provide another interpretation of this test. We argue that testing whether the forecasts have value is the same as determining whether (in the sense of predicting the direction of change) the forecast differs significantly from a naive model that continuously predicts up (down). The profession now categorizes the various tests as measuring directional accuracy. This concept can be illustrated either when GDP or inflation predictions are made separately or when both variables are examined together.

One variable

Most macroeconomic forecast evaluations focus on GDP and inflation. Basically, when the real GDP and inflation forecasts are each evaluated separately, they are grouped into two categories. The GNP/GDP forecasts are categorized according to whether GDP growth was positive or negative, and the inflation categories depend on whether inflation increased or decreased.[5] A 2 × 2 contingency table is created that compares the predicted outcome of a variable with the actual outcome of that variable (Table 6.1).[6]

Table 6.1 The Relationship between Predicted and Actual Outcomes

	Actual outcome		
Predicted outcome	> 0	≤ 0	
$\Delta Y > 0$	$n1$	$N2 - n2$	n
≤ 0	$N1 - n1$	$n2$	$N - n$
	$N1$	$N2$	N

NOTE: N = total number of observations; $N1$ = number of observations where the actual change was positive; $N2$ = number of observations where the actual change was negative. Small n's represent the same variables but refer to predicted changes. Blank = not applicable.
SOURCE: Author's calculations.

For notation we have a total of N observations where for $n1$ of them both the actual and the predicted are positive and for $n2$ of them both the actual and the predicted are negative. We have n observations where the predicted outcome is positive and $N - n$ observations where the predicted outcome is negative (or zero). We also have $N1$ observations where the actual outcome is positive and $N2 = N - N1$ observations where the actual outcome is negative (or zero). The Pesaran-Timmerman (1992) statistic along with the chi-square and Fisher's exact test can be used to test this hypothesis.[7]

The Pesaran-Timmermann statistic for predictive performance for an $m \times m$ contingency table with a total of N observations is

$$S_n = \sqrt{N} V_n^{-1/2} S_n$$

where we have the following:

$$\hat{V}_n = \left(\frac{\partial f(P)}{\partial P} \right)_{P=\hat{P}} \hat{\Omega} \left(\frac{\partial f(P)}{\partial P} \right)_{P=\hat{P}} .$$

$\hat{P}_{ij} = n_{ij} / N$, where n_{ij} is the number of observations in the ij category of the contingency table. $\hat{\Omega} = \hat{\Psi} - \hat{P}\hat{P}'$, where $\hat{\Psi}$ is an $m^2 \times m^2$ diagonal matrix with the elements of $\hat{P}$ on the diagonal.

$$S_n = \sum_{i=1}^{m} \left(\hat{P}_{ii} - \hat{P}_{i0}\hat{P}_{0i} \right),$$

where $\hat{P}_{i0} = n_{i0} / N$.

$$\hat{P}_{0i} = n_{0i} / N,$$

where n_{i0} and n_{0i} represent the ith row and column totals, respectively.

Pesaran and Timmermann (1992) present their results based on the square of this test statistic in order to more easily compare it to the chi-square goodness of fit statistic. This test statistic has a chi-square distribution with one degree of freedom.

Several variables

All of the questions discussed above were concerned with evaluating the forecasts of one variable at a time. However, in preparing a particular macroeconomic forecast, individuals are concerned with the outlook for both the growth rate and the rate of inflation. The accuracy of this overall forecast thus depends on how well both variables are predicted simultaneously. Thus, it is necessary to use a different contingency table for evaluating the directional accuracy of these macroeconomic forecasts. Sinclair, Stekler, and Kitzinger (2010) show that the simultaneous directional accuracy of the two variables can be evaluated by using a 4 × 4 contingency table rather than the 2 × 2 table that had been used in assessing each variable individually.[8]

In the expanded 4 × 4 table, instead of simply being categorized based on the separate GDP growth or inflation predictions, forecasts about the state of the economy are grouped into four categories: 1) GDP growth positive, inflation increasing; 2) GDP growth positive, inflation decreasing; 3) GDP growth negative, inflation increasing; and 4) GDP growth negative, inflation decreasing. The statistical tests are generalized versions of those used when the forecasts were analyzed separately.[9] Table 6.2 illustrates a 4 × 4 contingency table when the directional accuracy of the GDP growth and inflation forecasts of the Federal Reserve are evaluated jointly.

Test statistics

The statistical methodology tests whether or not the forecasts predict the associated directions of change. There are at least three test statistics that can be used to test the hypothesis that the forecasts fail to predict the observed events.[10] Two test statistics focus on independence. These test statistics are the chi-square and Fisher's exact test. The Pesaran-Timmermann (1992) statistic specifically focuses on predictive failure. The forecasts are said to have value only if the null hypothesis of predictive failure is rejected. Pesaran and Timmermann's predictive-failure test is particularly useful in the case where we undertake a joint evaluation of GDP growth and inflation forecasts. Their test does not require that the two forecasts be independent of each other. Since output and inflation may be predicted from the same forecasting model, this is an important consideration. In this particular case, the probability of the pattern of these forecasts occurring by chance is less than 0.001.

Table 6.2 The 4 × 4 Contingency Table for the Zero-Month Lead

	Actual outcome			
Predicted outcome	ΔGDP > 0, Δinf > 0	ΔGDP > 0, Δinf $\leq$ 0	ΔGDP $\leq$ 0, Δinf > 0	ΔGDP $\leq$ 0, Δinf $\leq$ 0
ΔGDP > 0, Δinf > 0	49	13	1	1
ΔGDP > 0, Δinf $\leq$ 0	7	43	0	4
ΔGDP $\leq$ 0, Δinf > 0	1	2	4	2
ΔGDP $\leq$ 0, Δinf $\leq$ 0	0	3	5	4

SOURCE: Sinclair, Stekler, and Kitzinger (2010).

Sinclair, Stekler, and Kitzinger (2010) thus conclude that the Fed forecasts for the current quarter yield an accurate view of the state of the economy.

Policy Forecast Errors: An Example

In general, to obtain a quantitative measure of the economic costs of forecast errors, the decision rule of the user of the prediction must be known, but it generally is not known. However, there is at least one case where the cost of forecast errors can be measured without knowing an explicit decision rule because there is another criterion for evaluating forecasts: are financial market and betting market decisions based on those forecasts profitable (Leitch and Tanner 1991)?

Macroeconomic forecasts, however, cannot be evaluated in this way, because there is no generally acceptable way of calculating their value to policymakers. There is an exception if the rule guiding policy decisions is known. Sinclair et al. (2009) show that it is possible to evaluate the quantitative forecasts of the Federal Reserve within the context of the Taylor Rule, which is assumed to be the one that guides the Fed in setting monetary policy.[11] The assumption is that the Fed's forecasts of multiple series are usually generated for a specific policy purpose, as inputs for monetary policy. In this case, an assessment of the quality of the quantitative forecasts of two or more variables depends on the relative importance of each to the Fed.

Specifically, let $P_{t,t+h}^f$ be a policy decision at time t that is a linear function of the h-step-ahead forecasts of $N \geq 1$ variables $(x_{i,t+h}^f, i=1,...N)$. The superscript f indicates that the policy decision is based on forecasts rather than on the actual outcomes of the variables:

(6.5) $\quad P_{t,t+h}^f = p(x_{1,t+h}^f,...x_{N,t+h}^f)$.

If policymakers had perfect foresight, the policy decision would simply be P_t, without the superscript f:

(6.6) $\quad P_{t,t+h} = p(x_{1,t+h},...x_{N,t+h})$.

However, because policy is based on forecasts, rather than on the actual data, policy is subject to errors that are functions of the mistakes made in forecasting the underlying variables $x_{i,t}$, $i = 1,...N$. The difference between the actual policy and the policy that would have been pursued under perfect foresight is called the policy forecast error (PFE):

$$(6.7) \quad PFE_t = P_{t,t+h} - P_{t,t+h}^f = p(x_{1,t+h},...x_{N,t+h}) - p(x_{1,t+h}^f,...x_{N,t+h}^f)$$

$$= e(e_{1,t+h},...e_{N,t+h}),$$

where $e_{1,t+h},...e_{N,t+h}$ are the forecast errors associated with the individual series. Thus the PFE is composed of the individual forecast errors weighted by their importance in the policy rule. According to the forward-looking Taylor rule,[12] the Fed sets a target federal funds rate, i_t^{Tf}, based on Equation (6.8), where, as above, the superscript f denotes that the target is based on forecast variables.[13] The Fed's policy decision $(P_{t,t+h}^f)$ is written as

$$(6.8) \quad P_{t,t+h}^f = i_t^{Tf} = r* + \pi_{t+h}^f + 0.5(\pi_{t+h}^f - \pi*) + 0.5(y_{t+h}^f - y*),$$

where $r*$ is the equilibrium real interest rate, $\pi*$ is the Fed's implicit inflation rate target, and $y*$ is the potential output growth rate.[14]

The actual outcome in period $t + h$, however, may differ from the Fed's forecasts. Therefore, if the members of the FOMC had known the actual values for π_{t+h} and y_{t+h} (i.e., if they had perfect forecasts or perfect foresight), they would have chosen a (potentially different) federal funds rate. Consequently, their policy decision under perfect foresight $(P_{t,t+h})$ would have been

$$(6.9) \quad P_{t,t+h} = i_t^T = r* + \pi_{t+h}^A + 0.5(\pi_{t+h}^A - \pi*) + 0.5(y_{t+h}^A - y*),$$

where π_{t+h}^A and y_{t+h}^A represent the actual realizations of π_{t+h} and y_{t+h}. The difference between i^{Tf} and i^T measures the difference in the federal funds rate that occurs because of inaccurate forecasts of output growth and inflation and thus represents the Federal Reserve's policy forecast error, PFE_t:

$$(6.10) \quad PFE_t = i_t^T - i_t^{Tf} = 1.5\left(\pi_{t+h}^A - \pi_{t+h}^f\right) + 0.5\left(y_{t+h}^A - y_{t+h}^f\right).$$

The differences, $\left(\pi_{t+h}^A - \pi_{t+h}^f\right)$ and $\left(y_{t+h}^A - y_{t+h}^f\right)$, are the Fed's forecast errors for the inflation rate and real output growth, respectively.

Given the PFEs, the evaluation procedures are similar to those used in judging individual forecast errors.

Using this methodology, Sinclair et al. (2009) were able to evaluate the impact that forecast errors had on the Fed's monetary policy as characterized by the Taylor rule. They found that the Fed's policy forecast error was in general unbiased and significantly smaller than the errors that would have resulted from naive forecasts, but not always significantly smaller than the errors that would have resulted from the SPF predictions. Nevertheless, the mean absolute policy forecast error of the Fed forecasts was approximately 1 percent (100 basis points).

FINDINGS FROM FORECAST EVALUATIONS (OF GDP GROWTH AND INFLATION)

There have been many studies that have reported on the accuracy of the forecasts of the growth of GDP and inflation. I have been involved in two survey papers that have summarized and synthesized the results of these studies. One looks at U.S. and U.K. forecasts (Fildes and Stekler 2002). The other docs a similar analysis of the G7 (excluding the U.S.) predictions (Stekler 2008). By comparing the forecasts of various countries, we can determine whether the findings are robust. The focus will be on five topics: 1) directional errors; 2) biases and systematic errors; 3) the magnitude of the errors; 4) the source of the errors; and 5) the trend, if any, in forecast accuracy.

Directional Errors

There are very few analyses about directional errors, because most forecast evaluations focus on the magnitude of the quantitative errors. However, Fildes and Stekler (2002) note that most U.S. and U.K. recessions were not predicted in advance, but neither did economists make many predictions of peaks that did not occur.[15] In a more recent study, Sinclair, Stekler, and Kitzinger (2010) analyze the directional accuracy of the Fed's forecasts of GDP and inflation and show that the predictions of increases and decreases in the inflation rate are not associated with the actual changes in that rate. When, however, the directional accuracy of the GDP and inflation predictions were analyzed jointly, on average the Fed's forecasts for the current quarter and the one-quarter-ahead period yielded an accurate view of the state of the economy.

The record for other countries is no better. The turning points in German GDP were not predicted, but the accelerations and decelerations of the growth rate were forecast accurately. (Stekler [2008] summarizes the literature relating to the forecasts of the G7 countries and indicates that the results apply equally to private forecasters, research institutes, and international organizations.) The evidence suggests that forecasters are not able to predict turning points in advance and may even have difficulty in detecting them quickly once they have occurred.

Biases and Systematic Errors

Most evaluations examine the rationality and efficiency of the predictions in order to determine whether they could have been improved. Stekler (2002) reviews a large number of studies and concludes that there is no definitive evidence that the U.S. inflation forecasts display weak-form informational efficiency. While more of the U.S. growth forecasts did not reject the null of informational efficiency, these results were also mixed.[16] The results were dependent on the database that was examined, the years that were examined, and the methodology that was employed. However, most of these analyses did not test whether the forecasts were truly inefficient or whether the errors could be attributable to asymmetric loss functions.

Forecasters also made systematic errors. They overestimated the rate of growth during slowdowns and underestimated it during recoveries and booms. Similarly, inflation was underpredicted when it was rising and overpredicted when it was declining. (See the surveys of Fildes and Stekler [2002] and Stekler [2008] for the specific studies from which these results were obtained.) Fildes and Stekler conclude, "These errors occurred when the economy was subject to major perturbations, just the time when accurate forecasts were most needed" (p.442).

Magnitude of the Errors

Although these qualitative findings about directional and systematic errors are important to our understanding the forecasting process, most evaluations have also provided quantitative estimates of these errors. Fildes and Stekler (2002) report that the mean absolute error of annual U.S. and U.K. GDP growth forecasts is around 1 percent. Newer studies have found similar results for the G7 countries, but previously Öller and Barot (2000) had found that the errors were larger for some of the other European countries (Stekler 2008).

When quarterly GDP estimates were examined, the previous papers did not all use identical procedures for calculating the mean absolute errors.[17] Consequently, our findings are not as complete. We do know that there is a substantial improvement in accuracy when the forecasting task switches from predicting what will happen in the next quarter to estimating the level of activity in the current quarter. This is largely attributable to the availability of actual data for the current period.

The inflation forecasts seem to have improved. The earlier U.S. inflation forecasts had mean absolute errors between 1.0 and 1.4 percent, but Stekler's (2008) survey of G7 forecasts shows that those errors are now between 0.5 and 0.75 percent. The reduction may be attributable to the lower inflation rates that have been observed in the past several decades.

Have the Forecasts Improved?

Given the number of papers that have evaluated macroeconomic forecasts, it is surprising how few have asked whether the quality of the predictions has improved over time. The problem is not the lack of data, for we have 40 years' worth of forecasts for some countries. However, the findings of those studies that have examined this issue are contradictory, and thus there are no definitive conclusions. For example, Heilemann and Stekler (2003) examine German forecasts and adjust the errors for the difficulties in predicting the relevant periods, but the results are mixed. Dopke and Fritsche (2006) also look at German forecasts and suggest that accuracy may have improved. As for the predictions of international organizations, Vogel (2007) shows that the accuracy of the OECD forecasts has improved, but Timmerman (2007) indicates that the quality of the International Monetary Fund forecasts has deteriorated. These findings are consistent with those summarized by Fildes and Stekler (2002). We conclude that despite all the resources that have been devoted to forecasting, there is no clear evidence that accuracy has improved.

This finding suggests that we may have reached the limits of forecastability. Heilemann and Stekler (2003) have investigated this hypothesis. We calculated the ex post forecast errors generated by simulations obtained from econometric models. These models can serve as a benchmark of the maximum accuracy that is attainable because they are free from errors caused by wrong assumptions about the predetermined variables and the inability to capture the dynamics of multiperiod forecasts. We find that the model's inflation errors are very similar to those that were made ex ante for the same period. This result indicates that the accuracy of the inflation forecasts could not have been improved substantially. On the other hand, the model's growth rate errors are substantially smaller than the ex ante errors, suggesting that the quality of the ex ante real-sector forecasts can still be improved.

Sources of Error: Recessions

A model-based forecast can be decomposed into various sources. The forecast depends upon the econometric specification, the exogenous variables and the corresponding predictions of these variables, and any adjustment that the economist makes to the model output. There are analytical difficulties associated with determining why each of these errors occurred. One example of this difficulty occurs when econometricians make assumptions about the exogenous variables rather than model adjustments to subjectively influence their forecasts.

Nevertheless, there is agreement that recessions are a significant cause of some of these errors. A large portion of GDP forecast errors are attributable to the failure to predict the occurrence of recessions. If recessions and booms are caused by events such as changes in asset prices that, it is assumed, cannot be predicted, then the recessions are themselves unforecastable. Fair (2009) finds that, ex post, some recessions could be predicted even if some key exogenous asset variables were estimated using only baseline paths.[18] The failure to adequately predict the other recessions could be explained by the inability to estimate some or all of these key exogenous variables.

What Have We Learned?

The evidence about the macro forecasts that has been presented here is very robust.[19] The findings of Fildes and Stekler (2002) that primarily related only to U.S. and U.K. forecasters are similar to those relating to the G7 economists. Both types of studies find that recessions are not predicted in advance and account for a significant portion of the quantitative errors. Neither type of study is able to show that forecast accuracy had improved, and both find that there were systematic errors. There may be a quantitative limit beyond which forecast accuracy cannot be improved (Heilemann and Stekler 2003).

Finally, we now have a somewhat better understanding of the forecasting process. We have learned that forecasts for a horizon longer than 12–18 months might not be valuable (Isiklar and Lahiri 2007; Vuchelen and Gutierrez 2005). We also know more about the causes of bias. Batchelor (2007) shows how the systematic errors or "biases" are related to the forecasters' optimism (or pessimism) and conservatism in revising their predictions. He notes that standard rationality tests are not appropriate if there has been a structural break. The pattern of the errors can then provide a way of understanding the forecasters' learning process about the impact of this structural break. Isiklar and Lahiri (2007) use forecast revisions to explain the behavioral characteristics of forecasters—i.e., how do they react to news and when is news important?[20] We know that there is much more work to be done in determining the importance of asymmetric losses, the sources of biases, the limits of accuracy, etc. Much can be learned about the sources of error if we undertake more studies like Heilemann's (2002).

LABOR MARKET FORECASTS

We now turn to a discussion of labor market forecasts. There are many fewer studies of these types of forecasts. Consequently, our results will be less informative. Before I discuss the results of evaluations of the forecasts of these variables, I want to briefly note that several labor market series are used as indicators or predictors about the overall state of the economy. These are outlined in the next section. Next

I consider the short-run quantitative forecasts of the U.S. unemployment rate. Finally, I consider long-run projections and the procedures for evaluating them. I also show that the methodology for evaluating long-run labor market forecasts can be used to analyze other types of long-run projections.

Labor Market Series as Indicators

The U.S. unemployment rate moves countercyclically and may display an asymmetric relationship with changes in GDP. It may have a short lead (or be coincident) at business cycle peaks, but it lags at the troughs (Montgomery et al. 1998). The unemployment rate is not considered either a leading or a coincident indicator. There are, however, two other series that are considered leading indicators of cyclical movements and one series that is considered a coincident indicator. These are series that are included in the various indicator indexes currently compiled and published by the Conference Board.

The two leading series are 1) average weekly hours in manufacturing and 2) average weekly claims for unemployment insurance.[21] While Diebold and Rudebusch (1989, 1991) have evaluated the composite leading indicators, I have found only one paper that examined the forecasting behavior of either of those series—Seip and McNown (2007). Seip and McNown examined the behavior of average weekly hours, but their analysis produced contradictory findings. For example, they examined the Granger causality between movements in the weekly hours series and changes in the Federal Reserve Board Index of Industrial Production. Their results show that the hours series is a lagging indicator with respect to the Index of Production, which is a coincident indicator. On the other hand, using sophisticated phase analysis, they find that the timing at turning points suggests that it is a leading indicator, but not that accurate of one.

It is possible that there may be another labor market series that could be a leading indicator. The official U.S. unemployment rate series is not the only measure of labor slack in the economy; the U.S. Department of Labor also compiles other measures of unemployment. The official or conventional unemployment rate is called U3 and measures the total number of unemployed persons as a percentage of the civilian labor force. The broadest BLS measure of unemployment is called U6.

It includes two additional categories: 1) people who have left the labor force because they have become discouraged at failing to find employment and 2) individuals who are working part time but would prefer to be full-time employees.

The difference between the two rates, therefore, represents the degree of labor underutilization that is not captured by the traditional unemployment rate. Figure 6.1 displays the difference between the U6 and U3 series and seems to indicate that this difference becomes larger before the cyclical turns of the U.S. business cycles for the period 1970–2009. The NBER-dated recessions are shaded. However, there has been no rigorous and systematic evaluation of this series to determine whether, in fact, this series is an adequate leading indicator.

The Conference Board also compiles and publishes a composite index of coincident series. The movements in this index roughly track the cyclical movements of the economy. There are four series in this composite index, with "employees on nonagricultural payrolls" representing the labor market. We should note the importance of using labor market data for forecasting cyclical movements, but the procedures for evaluating these time series as indicators are beyond the scope of this chapter.

Modeling and Forecasting the Unemployment Rate

Neftçi (1984) finds that the U.S. unemployment rate has an interesting characteristic: it displays asymmetric behavior because the probability of a decline following two previous declines differs from the probability of an increase given two prior increases. This suggests that a linear model would not adequately explain the behavior of this series. Subsequently, a number of univariate nonlinear models were developed to explain and then forecast this series.[22] More recently, Milas and Rothman (2008) go one step further by developing multivariate nonlinear models to explain the U.S. unemployment rate.

Only a small number of these nonlinear models have actually been used to forecast the U.S. unemployment rate. Rothman (1998) uses six models and, based on out-of-sample recursive simulations, concludes that their performance is better than that of a linear model.[23] Montgomery et al. (1998) undertake a more comprehensive evaluation. They use a threshold autoregressive (TAR) model to generate simulated

Figure 6.1 Difference between U6 and U3, 1970–2009

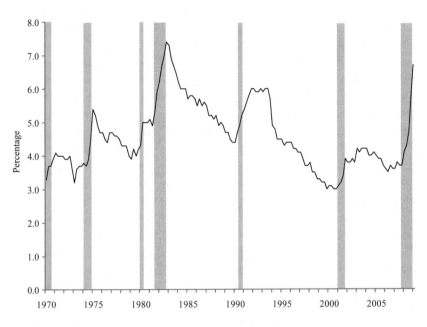

NOTE: U3 = The percentage of U.S. workers unemployed according to the conventional measure. U6 = The percentage of those people plus two other categories: 1) people who have left the labor force because they became discouraged at not finding work and 2) people working part time who would prefer to be working full time. The NBER-dated recessions are shaded.
SOURCE: Dougherty (2009).

recursive forecasts. These forecasts displayed smaller errors than were generated by the linear ARIMA model. Moreover, although no formal statistical tests were used, the forecasts of the TAR model appeared to be unbiased. Similarly, neural network models (Moshiri and Brown 2004) and nonparametric nonlinear models (Golan and Perloff 2004) were superior to linear models in forecasting the unemployment rate. In fact, Golan and Perloff indicate that their model is superior to the nonlinear TAR model.

Unfortunately, it is unlikely that any of these models will become the standard methodology for forecasting the unemployment rate. The median SPF forecast was more accurate than either the TAR or the nonparametric nonlinear models. In addition, Golan and Perloff find that the Michigan structural model also generated smaller errors.

Given these results, it is appropriate to also report some findings about nonmodel forecasts of the unemployment rate. The median SPF forecast was not only more accurate than the model predictions, but it was also superior to the Federal Reserve's *Greenbook* estimates for the period 1983–2004 (Baghestani 2008). The SPF errors are asymmetric, with mean errors during expansions amounting to less than 0.1 percent, while during recessions those errors sometimes exceed 1.0 percent (Montgomery et al. 1998). The Greenbook estimates are unbiased, but the errors are also asymmetric (Sinclair, Stekler, and Joutz 2008).

There is additional information about the quality of nonmodel unemployment rate forecasts. Carroll (2003) notes that the SPF forecasts were more accurate than those obtained from the Michigan Household Surveys (MHS). The MHS eventually did update its forecasts to conform to those of the professional forecasters. Professional forecasters' estimates of the unemployment rate were also consistent with Okun's Law, given their predictions of the change in real GDP (Pierdzioch, Rülke, and Stadtmann 2011).

These results suggest that we economists recognize the asymmetric behavior of the unemployment rate but have not yet been able to develop an appropriate model that captures the asymmetries better than our judgment does.

Long-Term Labor Market Forecasts: Methodology

The Bureau of Labor Statistics makes long-run projections of a number of variables. The variables include the size of the labor force, employment by industry, and employment by occupation. Because the projections are for a horizon of 10 or more years, they may be evaluated differently from analyses of short-term macroeconomic predictions. For example, an evaluation of these BLS long-term projections poses three methodological issues that usually are not encountered in analyses of short-term macroeconomic forecasts.

First, no other organization made projections of these variables. Consequently, there is no benchmark for judging the BLS forecasts. Second, these projections are long-term, not the short-term macroeconomic forecasts that have been evaluated in the past. Thus, the questions that must be addressed in such an evaluation can differ from those addressed in the macro forecasts. Finally, such a projection is a one-time forecast.[24] I will illustrate these issues with an example and show how the labor-force, employment-by-industry, and occupation projections that BLS made in 1989 for the year 2000 were evaluated (Stekler and Thomas 2005). Although these forecasts had already been evaluated individually (Fullerton 2003), it was possible both to ask additional questions that had not been addressed in earlier studies and to use evaluation methodologies different from those employed previously.

Benchmarks

There are no other forecasts that are comparable to the BLS projections; it is, therefore, necessary to construct a benchmark for the projections of each variable. In each case, BLS projections are compared with similar data obtained from the forecasts of these benchmarks. The benchmarks that were selected all use data that were available at the time when the BLS projections were prepared. In actuality, the benchmarks are taken from one of two naive models that are either 1) projecting the latest available information or 2) predicting that the change over the forecast period is equal to that observed over the previous time interval, which is of the same length as the forecast period.[25] The projections that are being analyzed in this article were prepared in 1988; thus the forecast period is 12 years in length. Consequently, the change from 1976 to 1988 was used as the benchmark here. At a minimum, the BLS projections should be more accurate than the forecasts of these naive models.

Questions in evaluating long-term projections versus short-term forecasts

The questions that are appropriate for evaluating the short-term forecasts have been examined in detail, but the questions that should be asked in analyzing longer-run projections have not been given the same degree of attention. Because BLS projections primarily focus on long-run trends, the questions asked and the statistics used in evaluating these forecasts should be related to the primary emphasis of the forecast.

Thus, the two basic questions to be asked in evaluating these projections are as follows:

1)   Have the trends, specifically structural changes, been predicted correctly? and

2)   Were these forecasts better than those that could have been produced by a benchmark method?

Additional questions concerning the sources of the errors and whether the forecasts improved over time can also be posed.

The statistics that can answer these questions include the following four:

1)   the percentage of components where the direction of change was predicted correctly;

2)   dissimilarity indexes that measure the structure of the labor force;

3)   contingency tables that determine whether the actual and predicted directions of change are related; and

4)   Spearman's rank correlation coefficients, which measure the relationship between the predicted and actual changes in the components of an aggregate forecast.

Questions about the labor force projection are listed in Table 6.3.[26] These include the following four:

1)   What is the projected size of the labor force, by age and gender?

2)   What is the growth rate of the labor force?

3)   What are the participation rates of the various groups? and

4)   What is the distribution of the total labor force by age and gender?

The error measures that were used in evaluating these projections are also presented in Table 6.3. They include the direction of error, the absolute and percentage error, the dissimilarity index, etc. The limitations of these questions and statistics are also noted.

Measuring structural change: dissimilarity indexes

In order to determine whether the structural changes and major trends that occurred between 1988 and 2000 were predicted accurately, a statistic is used that directly addresses this question. The forecast of the total labor force is an aggregated estimate, and it is important to also examine the disaggregated component predictions. Such an analysis enables one to determine whether the structure of the aggregate has been predicted accurately—i.e., whether the distribution of the labor force across various categories is accurate.

If the aggregate, X, is predicted according to some scenario (for example, full employment), one would want to determine whether the structure is accurate even if the total is wrong. Kolb and Stekler (1992) developed a procedure for decomposing the total error into two components, where the first measures the scenario discrepancy and the second the structural error. They calculated the proportion of the aggregate predicted and actual totals that were associated with each of the i components. While their analysis was based on an information-content statistic, using dissimilarity indexes would yield the same result.

A dissimilarity index is a statistic that can be used to determine whether one distribution approximates another one. Specifically, it measures the amount by which the forecasted distribution would have to change to be identical to the actual distribution. The formula for the dissimilarity index is

$$(6.11) \quad D = 0.5 \sum | (P_{fi} / P_f) - (P_{ai} / P_a) | ,$$

where P_{fi} is the forecast proportion of the labor force that will be in the ith group, and P_f is the forecast for the total labor force. Similarly, P_{ai} and P_a are the corresponding actual data. D is bounded in the interval of 0 to 100 percent. The smaller the value of D, the smaller the difference between the predicted and actual distributions—that is, the more accurate the forecast.

The dissimilarity index for the BLS labor force projections was based on the 14 age/gender categories that had been used in 1989 to prepare the estimates for 2000. Similar dissimilarity indexes were constructed for the other distributions that serve as standards of comparison. The values of the various dissimilarity indexes are presented

Table 6.3 Questions Asked about the Labor Force Forecasts

Questions	Accuracy measure	Problem with measure or question	New question or measure
What is the size of the total labor force?	Mean absolute error; percentage error; direction of error	Does not distinguish between census population errors and participation rate errors; no standard of comparison	How much of total labor force error is the result of participation rate errors? Standard of comparison: 1988 participation rates
What is the size of the labor force by gender?	Mean absolute error; percentage error; direction of error	Same as total labor force	Same as total labor force
What is the growth rate of the total labor force?	Error in percentage points	Same as total labor force	How much of the error in the growth rate forecast is the result of participation rate errors? Standard of comparison: 1988 participation rates
What are the participation rates of total labor force? Of men? Of women? By age and sex?	Error in percentage points, or absolute error/participation rate; mean absolute percentage error	Does not indicate whether direction of change in participation rate was predicted; no standard of comparison	Were the directions of change in the participation rates accurately predicted? Standard of comparison: number of changes accurately predicted vs. predictions by chance (binomial, $p = 0.5$)

What is the distribution of the labor force by age and sex?	No standard of comparison	Comparison standard: dissimilarity index based on 1988 distribution
	—	

NOTE: — = no established accuracy measure.
SOURCE: Stekler and Thomas (2005).

in Appendix Table 6A.3. The benchmarks were the projections based on various estimates of the population and alternative estimates of the participation rates.

The results are mixed. In some cases, the dissimilarity indexes obtained from the BLS projections are smaller (and thus more accurate) than those of the standards of comparison. In other cases, the opposite results were obtained. However, the dissimilarity index for the actual BLS forecast never exceeds 2 percent for any age/gender category or for men or women separately. The values of the dissimilarity indexes of the standards of comparison were comparable. While there is no statistical distribution for the dissimilarity index, the BLS projection substantially predicted the structural changes that occurred in the labor force between 1988 and 2000. On the other hand, similar results were obtained from the naive models that served as the benchmarks.

Similar procedures were used to evaluate the employment-by-industry and occupational projections. The BLS employment and naive projections were again similar, but the BLS occupational estimates were more accurate than the naive benchmark. Stekler and Thomas (2005) conclude that the accuracy of the BLS projections are comparable to the estimates obtained from naive extrapolative methods.

The applicability of the long-term evaluation methodology

The methodology that was applied in evaluating the BLS long-term projections has not been widely used. I want to show that it has a wider applicability by evaluating some long-run census population projections. One benefit of this analysis is the existence of multiple projections for a given date, permitting us to determine how the accuracy changes with a reduction in the forecast horizon.

The Census Bureau makes periodic forecasts of the population of the United States 5, 10, or more years into the future. These forecasts are both for the total U.S. population and for the number of inhabitants of each of the states. There have been many evaluations of these state forecasts (e.g., Campbell 2002; Smith and Sincich 1990, 1992; Wang 2002). In all cases, the error measures were based on the magnitude of the discrepancies between the projected and actual state population figures.

In addition to statistics that measure the quantitative errors, one can use the methodology that was applied to the BLS projections for these census data. One of the purposes of a long-range projection of each state's population is to provide a picture of the distribution of the aggregate U.S. population among the various states. If one were only interested in knowing whether the projections captured the important trends that actually occurred, one might not be concerned with the magnitude of the errors. The accuracy of the quantitative projections of each state's total population is then not as relevant.

It is possible that the share of the nation's population that was in each state was predicted correctly, but that the national total and the estimates for each of the states were inaccurate by the same proportion. In that case, the projected distribution of the state populations would have exactly matched the observed distribution. Thus, the evaluation procedure that is suggested here does not focus on the specific numbers in the projections or the magnitude of the misestimates. Rather, this evaluation asks whether the projected share of the total U.S. population by state was similar to the actual distribution. Such an analysis enables one to determine whether the state distribution of the aggregate population was accurate even if the aggregate estimate is inaccurate.

Decomposing the errors. Assume that x_t^a is the actual aggregate population of the United States at time t and x_t^f is the aggregate value that was projected for time t. The error in the aggregate projection is

$$(6.12) \quad e_t = x_t^a - x_t^f.$$

In addition, it is possible to examine the errors associated with the population projections for each of the i states. Accordingly, the proportions of the forecasted (f_i) and actual (a_i) aggregated population associated with each of the i states are

$$x_{i,t}^f = (f_{i,t})x_t^f \, ; \qquad x_{i,t}^a = (a_{i,t})x_t^a; \qquad \sum f_{i,t} = 1; \qquad \sum a_{i,t} = 1 \, ;$$

and the forecast error for each state is

$$(6.14) \quad e_{i,t} = (a_{i,t})x_t^a - (f_{i,t})x_t^f.$$

If the aggregate forecast is absolutely accurate, the quantitative error for each state would be

$$(6.15) \quad e_{i,t} = (a_{i,t} - f_{i,t})x_{i,t}^a,$$

which is the difference between the actual and forecast proportions of the aggregate population in each state. The same holds true if the aggregate forecast is inaccurate. If $x_t^a \neq x_t^f$,

$$(6.16) \quad e_{i,t} = (a_{i,t} - f_{i,t})x_t^a + f_{i,t}(x_t^a - x_t^f).$$

Thus the quantitative forecast error for each state, $e_{i,t}$, is the sum of two components. The first represents the error in predicting the proportion of the population in each state. The second measures the error in failing to predict the aggregate correctly. In order to evaluate these long-term population forecasts, we will focus on the first term, using the dissimilarity measure as our statistic.

The alternative methodology (benchmark) in this case is a naive model, because a valid forecasting procedure should be as accurate as this type of model. In this case, we assume that the naive projection of the states' shares of the U.S. population for year $t + h$ is identical to the known distribution that is available from either the census count or from the population estimate in year t, the year from which the projection was extended.

Data. We evaluate the census state population projections that were made between 1970 and 1996 for the years 1975–2005.[27] There are seven such sets of projections. The length of the forecasting horizon varied between 2 and 25 years. The naive projections were made using the same starting points and horizons. These projections were compared either with the actual census counts for 1980, 1990, and 2000 or with the population estimates that the Census Bureau made for 1975, 1985, 1995, and 2005.

Results. The dissimilarity indexes derived from both the census and naive projections are presented in Table 6.4. The longer the projection horizon, the larger the size of the dissimilarity index that was associated with the projections—i.e., the less accurate the projected

Table 6.4 Values of Dissimilarity Index (%) for Census and Naive Forecasts

Year projections made	Year of projection						
	1975	1980	1985	1990	1995	2000	2005
1970	a 1.7	a 3.9	a 5.5	a 6.5			
	b 1.7	b 3.9	b 5.5	b 6.4			
	[0.2]	[0.4]	[0.7]	[0.8]			
1975		1.8		3.7		5.3	
		[2.7]		[0.7]		[0.9]	
1980				2.5		4.2	
				[0.4]		[0.7]	
1986				1.0	1.2	1.9	2.3
				[0.2]	[0.3]	[0.4]	[0.4]
1988				a 0.6		a 2.5	
				b 0.8		b 1.7	
				[0.1]		[0.4]	
1992					0.4	1.4	2.0
					[0.1]	[0.2]	[0.4]
1996						0.8	1.2
						[0.2]	[0.3]

NOTE: Numbers in brackets are for naive (benchmark) projections. There were two sets of census projections issued in 1970 and 1988. They are denoted "a" and "b."
SOURCE: Author's calculations.

distribution. This result is similar to findings about the relationship between quantitative errors and the length of the horizon in short-run forecasts. As indicated above, the size of these indexes measures the amount by which the projected distribution would have to change to be identical to the actual distribution. This ranged from less than 1 percent for the very short projections to more than 5 percent for some of the longer horizons.

Moreover, the projections seem to have improved over time. For the five-year projections, the values of the dissimilarity indexes declined from more than 1.5 percent to less than 1 percent. The magnitude of the index for the ten-year projection made in 1970 was almost 4 percent; the similar measurements for the projections made in the late 1980s and

1990s were all less than 1.5 percent. A similar trend was observed in the more recent twenty-year projections.

Nevertheless, the census forecasts associated with the distributions of the state population forecasts are inferior to the naive forecasts (Table 6.4). In all but one case, the dissimilarity indexes associated with the naive forecasts are smaller than the ones derived from the comparable census projections. The exception is the five-year projection made in 1975.

CONCLUSIONS

In providing these perspectives on forecast evaluations, I started with questions that were posed 20 years ago. While the nomenclature may have changed, we still ask the same questions today. On the other hand, the statistical and econometric foundations of our analyses have been vastly improved, and new methodologies for forecasting have been developed.

Despite all these efforts, there are not many positive results to report about the quality of our forecasting techniques. We do know that combining forecasts tends to improve accuracy. We also can test for the limits of forecastability and can determine whether we have achieved that limit yet.

On the negative side, our results on the question of whether the accuracy of our forecasts has improved over time are ambiguous. We still fail to predict turning points, and the short-run forecasts still display biases and inefficiencies. The limited amount of evidence about long-run labor market and population projections suggests that, in some dimensions, they are no better than naive models.

However, we should not despair but rather focus on another aspect of these results. We still have immense opportunities for productive research. Let me suggest a few entries in a laundry list of possible research topics.

- How can we improve our forecasting models?
- Using these models, what are the limits of forecastability?
- How does one predict turning points?

- Why do economists prefer failing to forecast a turn that occurs rather than predicting a turn that does not happen?

- How valuable are indicators?

- Do forecasters have asymmetric loss functions?

- How are expectations (forecasts) formed?

- How do individuals go about making and revising their forecasts?

- What are the appropriate techniques for evaluating multivariate forecasts?

- For evaluating long-run predictions?

- For evaluating probability forecasts such as those contained in fan charts?

- How valuable are market-based (futures) forecasts?

- Finally, to what extent do real-time data problems affect our predictive accuracy?

To answer these questions, many more studies, such as those cited here, are required. It will obviously take time to answer all of these questions, but the results should provide a substantial payoff in increased forecast accuracy.

Notes

1. West (2006) has still another view about forecast evaluation: he argues that these evaluations provide inferences about the characteristics of models. Thus the focus is exclusively on forecasts generated by models, whether in sample or out of sample.

2. In that regard, the aforementioned econometric procedures for conducting evaluations provide a rigorous theoretical methodology for the statistical measures.

3. The mean square error criterion is associated with a quadratic loss function. (See Elliott and Timmermann 2008.) Another metric is mean absolute error.

4. This method can also be applied to one forecaster making several forecasts for the same horizon. (See Clements, Joutz, and Stekler 2007.)

5. No change is classified with the negative changes. Note that we are focusing on the direction of change in the inflation rate, which is equivalent to measuring accelerations and decelerations of the price level.

6. The contingency table methodology is used to test whether the sign of the predicted change is probabilistically independent of the sign of the actual change.

This is also a test of the hypothesis that the forecasts are more accurate than those of a naive random-walk model in predicting the direction of change. (See Stekler 1994, p. 497.)

7. The chi-square and Fisher's exact test are well known and are not presented here.

8. Naik and Leuthold (1986) also use a 4 × 4 contingency table in their qualitative analysis of forecasting performance. Their study focuses on a different topic—the ability to predict turning points. (Also see Kaylen and Brandt 1988.)

9. There is, however, a difference in interpretation once we go beyond the simple 2 × 2 case. In particular, the 2 × 2 contingency table tests for predictive failure of only one variable, whereas the 4 × 4 contingency table tests for predictive failure of both variables. Moreover, in the 2 × 2 case, the hypothesis of predictive failure is equivalent to the hypothesis that the actual and predicted values of the variable are independent of each other. As discussed in Pesaran and Timmermann (1992), however, for the 4 × 4 case they are no longer equivalent. For our contingency table, independence implies predictive failure, but not vice versa.

10. Merton (1981) and Henriksson and Merton (1981) use a test based on the hypergeometric distribution. This is identical to Fisher's exact test. Their test assumes known row and column frequencies, which is not assumed for the Pesaran-Timmermann test.

11. The literature assumes that the Taylor rule is an approximation to the decision rule of the Fed. Also note that this procedure is in the framework of a decision-based forecast evaluation, discussed above.

12. Although Taylor (1993) originally proposed his rule as an empirical description of past Fed policy actions, Woodford (2001a,b) has shown that the Taylor rule can also be justified based on a firm theoretical foundation.

13. Following Orphanides (2001), we assume that the Fed uses the *Greenbook* forecasts in their decision rule. The members of the FOMC also make their own forecasts, but they have access to the staff forecasts of the *Greenbook* when doing so. For an evaluation of those forecasts, see Romer and Romer (2008).

14. While the output gap is typically used in the Taylor rule, the growth rate is typically used in forecast evaluation. The growth rate of the actuals is approximately $\ln(Y_t) - \ln(Y_{t-1})$, whereas the growth rate of the forecasts is approximately $\ln(Y_t^f) - \ln(Y_{t-1})$. Thus, when we subtract one from the other for the policy forecast error, we have $\ln(Y_t) - \ln(Y_t^f)$. Approximating the output gaps in the same manner, we have $\ln(Y_t) - \ln(Y^*)$ and $\ln(Y_t^f) - \ln(Y^*)$, so again we have $\ln(Y_t) - \ln(Y_t^f)$. It is this result that permits us to use the growth rate in order to construct the PFEs. This analysis does assume, however, that potential output, Y^*, is known rather than a forecast. This assumption is based on the lack of forecasts for this variable in the *Greenbook*. For a discussion of the role of real time output gap estimates and the Taylor rule, see Orphanides (2001).

15. The U.S. false turns predicted in 1978–1979 were an exception, but real GNP did decline for two quarters during this period.

16. The U.K. forecasts yielded similar results.

17. Some authors transform the errors into annual growth rates; others do not.

18. The exogenous asset variables in the Fair (2009) model are equity prices and housing prices. His simulations also assumed that import prices and exports as well as the asset variables could only be estimated using baseline benchmarks.

19. This summary refers only to the findings mentioned in the text. There are many other topics in the forecasting literature that were not reviewed and are beyond the scope of this paper. These include the quality of the data (Öller and Teterukovsky 2007), leading indicators (Allen and Morzuch 2006), and the role of judgmental forecasting (Lawrence et al. 2006). In addition, one could investigate the value of combining forecasts, the value of data revisions, and the question of which actuals to use in conducting an evaluation.

20. In the forecasts made for year t, the most important revisions occur at the end of $t-1$.

21. The Conference Board has constructed a Composite Leading Index, and these series are included in that index. They have also been included in earlier composite indexes that have been constructed by the U.S. Department of Commerce.

22. Skalin and Teräsvirta (2002) provide a list of studies that have employed nonlinear models to estimate unemployment rates. Swanson and White (1997) select models based on their ability to predict macroeconomic variables, including the unemployment rate, in real time. Clements and Krolzig (2003) survey the development of asymmetric business-cycle models and develop statistical tests but do not apply these models to U.S. unemployment data.

23. Pool and Speight (2000) had a similar finding for the U.K. and Japanese economies.

24. In most forecast evaluations, there is a time series of forecasts. It is then possible to discuss the characteristics of the average forecast. This is not possible with a single observation.

25. These benchmarks are identical to the ones used to calculate the U coefficients in short-run forecast evaluations.

26. The questions about occupation projections and employment are presented in Appendix Tables 6A.1 and 6A.2.

27. The data were obtained from U.S. Bureau of the Census, Current Population Reports, Series P25, Nos. 477, 735, 937, 1017, 1044, 1053, and 1111.

Appendix 6A
Questions about Forecasts, and Dissimilarity Indexes for Labor Force Projections

Table 6A.1 Questions about Occupational Forecasts

Question	Accuracy measure	Problem with question and/or accuracy measure	New question and/or measure
How many people will be employed in each occupation?	Absolute error; absolute percentage error	No standard of comparison; gives equal weight to large and small occupations	Standard of comparison: naive model—same growth; mean weighted percentage error
Which occupations will grow fastest?	Compare the number of occupations projected to grow the fastest with those that did grow fastest; distribution of growth rates by growth adjectives	No standard of comparison; no analysis of all occupations' projected and actual growth rates	Spearman's rank correlation coefficient; standard of comparison not possible because of definitional changes
Which occupations will have the largest job growth?	Compare the number of occupations that were projected to have largest job growth with those that did	No standard of comparison	Standard of comparison not possible because of definitional changes
What is the distribution of employment by occupation?	Absolute percentage error	No standard of comparison	Dissimilarity index: comparison with naive model

141

What were the sources of errors?	Model simulations	None

NOTE: Blank = not applicable.
SOURCE: Stekler and Thomas (2005).

Table 6A.2 Questions Asked about the Employment-by-Industry Forecasts

Questions	Accuracy measure	Problem with measure or question	New question or measure
How many people will be employed in each industry?	Percentage error; mean absolute percentage error	No standard of comparison; gives equal weight to large and small industries	Standard of comparison: rates of growth equal to previous rates of growth; mean weighted percentage error
Which industries would have the highest (lowest) employment growth rates?	Compare the number of industries projected to grow the fastest (slowest) with those that did grow fastest (slowest)	No standard of comparison; no analysis of all industries' projected and actual growth rates	Standard of comparison: forecasts of fastest- (slowest-) growing industries from naive model; Spearman's rank correlation coefficient for all industries
What is the distribution of employment by industry?	Dissimilarity index	No standard of comparison	Standard of comparison: same share as in 1988; shares are based on previous growth rates
What were the sources of the industry employment forecast errors?	Model simulations	None	

NOTE: Blank = not applicable.
SOURCE: Stekler and Thomas (2005).

Table 6A.3 Dissimilarity Indexes for Labor Force Projections (%)

BLS projections		Standards of comparison		
		Actual population and		Census population estimate and 1988 partic-ipation rate
		BLS partic-ipation rate	1988 partic-ipation rate	
Gender, age	1.83	2.02	2.24	2.32
Men, age	1.63	0.91	0.62	1.37
Women, age	1.91	2.86	2.40	1.32

NOTE: Numbers represent the dissimilarity indexes using alternative standards of comparison.
SOURCE: Author's calculations.

References

Allen, P. Geoffrey, and Bernard J. Morzuch. 2006. "Twenty-Five Years of Progress, Problems, and Conflicting Evidence in Econometric Forecasting. What about the Next 25 Years?" *International Journal of Forecasting* 22(3): 475–492.

Baghestani, Hamid. 2008. "Federal Reserve versus Private Information: Who Is the Best Unemployment Rate Predictor?" *Journal of Policy Modeling* 30(1): 101–110.

Batchelor, Roy A. 1990. "All Forecasters Are Equal." *Journal of Business and Economic Statistics* 8(1): 143–144.

———. 2007. "Bias in Macroeconomic Forecasts." *International Journal of Forecasting* 23(2): 189–203.

Campbell, Paul R. 2002. "Evaluating Forecast Error in State Population Projections Using Census 2000 Counts." Working Paper No. 57. Washington, DC: U.S. Census Bureau, Population Division.

Carroll, Christopher D. 2003. "Macroeconomic Expectations of Households and Professional Forecasters." *Quarterly Journal of Economics* 118(1): 269–298.

Clements, Michael P., Fred Joutz, and H.O. Stekler. 2007. "An Evaluation of the Forecasts of the Federal Reserve: A Pooled Approach." *Journal of Applied Econometrics* 22(1): 121–136.

Clements, Michael P., and Hans-Martin Krolzig. 2003. "Business Cycle Asymmetries: Characterization and Testing Based on Markov-Switching Autoregressions." *Journal of Business and Economic Statistics* 21(1): 196–211.

Davies, Anthony, and Kajal Lahiri. 1995. "A New Framework for Analyzing Survey Forecasts Using Three-Dimensional Panel Data." *Journal of Econometrics* 68(1): 205–227.

———. 1999. "Re-examining the Rational Expectations Hypothesis Using Panel Data on Multi-Period Forecasts." In *Analysis of Panels and Limited Dependent Variable Models*, Cheng Hsiao, Kajal Lahiri, Lung-Fei Lee, and M. Hashem Pesaran, eds. Cambridge: Cambridge University Press, pp. 226–254.

Diebold, Francis X., and Roberto S. Mariano. 1995. "Comparing Predictive Accuracy." *Journal of Business and Economic Statistics* 13(3): 253–263.

Diebold, Francis X., and Glenn D. Rudebusch. 1989. "Scoring the Leading Indicators." *Journal of Business* 62(3): 369–391.

———. 1991. "Forecasting Output with the Composite Leading Index: A Real-Time Analysis." *Journal of the American Statistical Association* 86(415): 603–610.

Döpke, Jörg, and Ulrich Fritsche. 2006. "Growth and Inflation Forecasts for Germany: A Panel-Based Assessment of Accuracy and Efficiency." *Empirical Economics* 31(3): 777–798.

Dougherty, John. 2009. "The U6 U3 Difference as a Turning Point Indicator." Photocopy. George Washington University, Washington, DC.

Elliott, Graham, and Allan Timmermann. 2008. "Economic Forecasting." *Journal of Economic Literature* 46(1): 3–56.

Fair, Ray C. 2009. "Analyzing Macroeconomic Forecastability." Cowles Foundation Discussion Paper No. 1706. New Haven, CT: Yale University.

Fildes, Robert, and H.O. Stekler. 2002. "The State of Macroeconomic Forecasting." *Journal of Macroeconomics* 24(4): 435–468.

Fullerton, Howard N. Jr. 2003. "Evaluating the BLS Labor Force Projections to 2000." *Monthly Labor Review* 126(10): 3–12.

Golan, Amos, and Jeffrey M. Perloff. 2004. "Superior Forecasts of the U.S. Unemployment Rate Using a Nonparametric Method." *Review of Economics and Statistics* 86(1): 433–438.

Harvey, David, Stephen Leybourne, and Paul Newbold. 1997. "Testing the Equality of Prediction Mean Squared Errors." *International Journal of Forecasting* 13(2): 281–291.

Heilemann, Ullrich. 2002. "Increasing the Transparency of Macroeconometric Forecasts: A Report from the Trenches." *International Journal of Forecasting* 18(1): 85–105.

Heilemann, Ullrich, and H.O. Stekler. 2003. "Has the Accuracy of German Macroeconomic Forecasts Improved?" Discussion paper of the German Research Council's research centre. Bonn: German Research Council.

Henriksson, R.D., and R.C. Merton. 1981. "On the Market Timing and Investment Performance of Managed Portfolios II: Statistical Procedures for Evaluating Forecasting Skills." *Journal of Business* 54(4): 513–533.

Holden, Kenneth, and David A. Peel. 1990. "On Testing for Unbiasedness and Efficiency of Forecasts." *Manchester School* 58(2): 120–127.

Isiklar, Gultekin, and Kajal Lahiri. 2007. "How Far Ahead Can We Forecast? Evidence from Cross-Country Surveys." *International Journal of Forecasting* 23(2): 167–187.

Kaylen, Michael S., and Jon A. Brandt. 1988. "A Note on Qualitative Forecast Evaluation: Comment." *American Journal of Agricultural Economics* 70(2): 415–416.

Kolb, R.A., and H.O. Stekler. 1992. "Information Content of Long-Term Employment Forecasts." *Applied Economics* 24(6): 593–596.

Lawrence, Michael, Paul Goodwin, Marcus O'Connor, and Dilek Onkal. 2006. "Judgmental Forecasting: A Review of Progress over the Last 25 Years." *International Journal of Forecasting* 22(3): 493–518.

Leitch, Gordon, and J. Ernest Tanner. 1991. "Economic Forecast Evaluation: Profit versus the Conventional Error Measures." *American Economic Review* 81(3): 580–590.

Merton, Robert C. 1981. "On Market Timing and Investment Performance: I— An Equilibrium Theory of Value for Market Forecasts." *Journal of Business* 54(3): 363–406.

Milas, Costas, and Philip Rothman. 2008. "Out-of-Sample Forecasting of Unemployment Rates with Pooled STVECM Forecasts." *International Journal of Forecasting* 24(1): 101–121.

Mincer, Jacob, and Victor Zarnowitz. 1969. "The Evaluation of Economic Forecasts." In *Economic Forecasts and Expectations: Analysis of Forecasting Behavior and Performance*, Jacob Mincer, ed. Cambridge, MA: National Bureau of Economic Research, pp. 1–46.

Montgomery, Alan L., Victor Zarnowitz, Ruey S. Tsay, and George C. Tiao. 1998. "Forecasting the U.S. Unemployment Rate." *Journal of the American Statistical Association* 93(442): 478–493.

Moshiri, Saeed, and Laura K. Brown. 2004. "Unemployment Variation over the Business Cycles: A Comparison of Forecasting Models." *Journal of Forecasting* 23(7): 497–511.

Naik, Gopal, and Raymond M. Leuthold. 1986. "A Note on Qualitative Forecast Evaluation." *American Journal of Agricultural Economics* 68(3): 721–726.

Neftçi, Salih N. 1984. "Are Economic Time Series Asymmetric over the Business Cycle?" *Journal of Political Economy* 92(2): 307–328.

Newey, Whitney K., and Kenneth D. West. 1987. "A Simple, Positive Semi-Definite, Heteroskedasticity and Autocorrelation Consistent Covariance Matrix." *Econometrica* 55(3): 703–708.

Öller, Lars-Erik, and Bharat Barot. 2000. "Comparing the Accuracy of European GDP Forecasts." *International Journal of Forecasting* 16(3): 293–315.

Öller, Lars-Erik, and Alex Teterukovsky. 2007. "Quantifying the Quality of Macroeconomic Variables." *International Journal of Forecasting* 23(2): 205–217.

Orphanides, Athanasios. 2001. "Monetary Policy Rules Based on Real-Time Data." *American Economic Review* 91(4): 964–985.

Pesaran, M. Hashem, and Spyros Skouras. 2002. "Decision-Based Methods for Forecast Evaluation." In *A Companion to Economic Forecasting*, Michael P. Clements and David F. Hendry, eds. Malden, MA: Blackwell, pp. 241–267.

Pesaran, M. Hashem, and Allan Timmermann. 1992. "A Simple Nonparametric Test of Predictive Performance." *Journal of Business and Economic Statistics* 10(4): 461–465.

Pierdzioch, Christian, Jan-Christoph Rülke, and Georg Stadtmann. 2011. "Do Professional Economists' Forecasts Reflect Okun's Law? Some Evidence for the G-7 Countries." *Applied Economics* 43(11): 1365–1373.

Pool, David A., and A.E.H. Speight. 2000. "Threshold Nonlinearities in Unemployment Rates: Further Evidence for the UK and G3 Economies." *Applied Economics* 32(6): 705–715.

Romer, Christina D., and David H. Romer. 2008. "The FOMC versus the Staff: Where Can Monetary Policymakers Add Value?" *American Economic Review* 98(2): 230–235.

Rothman, Philip. 1998. "Forecasting Asymmetric Unemployment Rates." *Review of Economics and Statistics* 80(1): 164–168.

Schnader, M.H., and H.O. Stekler. 1990. "Evaluating Predictions of Change." *Journal of Business* 63(1): 99–107.

Seip, Knut Lehre, and Robert McNown. 2007. "The Timing and Accuracy of Leading and Lagging Business Cycle Indicators: A New Approach." *International Journal of Forecasting* 23(2): 277–287.

Sinclair, Tara M., H.O. Stekler, and Fred Joutz. 2008. "Are 'Unbiased' Forecasts Really Unbiased? Another Look at the Fed Forecasts." IIEP Working Paper No. 6. Washington, DC: George Washington University, Institute for International Economic Policy.

Sinclair, Tara M., H.O Stekler, and Lindsay Kitzinger. 2010. "Directional Forecasts of GDP and Inflation: A Joint Evaluation with an Application to Federal Reserve Predictions." *Applied Economics* 42(18): 2289–2297.

Sinclair, Tara M., H.O. Stekler, Elizabeth Reid, and Edward N. Gamber. 2009. "Jointly Evaluating GDP and Inflation Forecasts in the Context of the Taylor Rule." IIEP Working Paper No. 2008-5. Washington, DC: George Washington University, Institute for International Economic Policy.

Skalin, Joakim, and Timo Teräsvirta. 2002. "Modeling Asymmetries and Moving Equilibria in Unemployment Rates." *Macroeconomic Dynamics* 6(2): 202–241.

Smith, Stanley K., and Terry Sincich. 1990. "The Relationship between the Length of the Base Period and Population Forecast Errors." *Journal of the American Statistical Association* 85(410): 367–375.

———. 1992. "Evaluating the Forecast Accuracy and Bias of Alternative Population Projections for States." *International Journal of Forecasting* 8(3): 495–508.

Stekler, H.O. 1991a. "Macroeconomic Forecast Evaluation Techniques." *International Journal of Forecasting* 7(3): 375–384.

———. 1991b. "Turning Point Predictions, Errors, and Procedures." In *Leading Economic Indicators: New Approaches and Forecasting Records,*

Kajal Lahiri and Geoffrey H. Moore, eds. Cambridge: Cambridge University Press, pp. 169–182.

———. 1994. "Are Economic Forecasts Valuable?" *Journal of Forecasting* 13(6): 495–505.

———. 2002. "The Rationality and Efficiency of Individuals' Forecasts." In *A Companion to Economic Forecasting*, Michael P. Clements and David F. Hendry, eds. Malden, MA: Blackwell, pp. 222–240.

———. 2008. "What Do We Know about G-7 Macro Forecasts?" In *Empirische Wirtschaftsforschung Heute*, Adolf Wagner, ed. Stuttgart, Germany: Schäffer-Poeschel, pp. 207–213.

Stekler, H.O., and Rupin Thomas. 2005. "Evaluating BLS Labor Force, Employment, and Occupation Projections for 2000." *Monthly Labor Review* 128(7): 46–56.

Swanson, Norman R., and Halbert White. 1997. "A Model Selection Approach to Real-Time Macroeconomic Forecasting Using Linear Models and Artificial Neural Networks." *Review of Economics and Statistics* 79(4): 540–550.

Taylor, John B. 1993. "Discretion versus Policy Rules in Practice." *Carnegie-Rochester Conference Series on Public Policy* 39(1): 195–214.

Timmermann, Allan. 2007. "An Evaluation of the *World Economic Outlook* Forecasts." *IMF Staff Papers* 54(1): 1–33.

Vogel, Lukas. 2007. "How Do the OECD Growth Projections for the G7 Economies Perform? A Post-Mortem." OECD Working Paper No. 573. Paris: Organisation for Economic Co-operation and Development.

Vuchelen, Jef, and Maria-Isabel Gutierrez. 2005. "Do the OECD 24-Month Horizon Growth Forecasts for the G7 Countries Contain Information?" *Applied Economics* 37(8): 855–862.

Wang, C. 2002. "Evaluation of Census Bureau's 1995–2005 State Population Projections." Working Paper No. 67. Washington, DC: U.S. Census Bureau.

West, Kenneth D. 2006. "Forecast Evaluation." In *Handbook of Economic Forecasting*, Vol. 1, Graham Elliott, Clive W.J. Granger, and Allan Timmermann, eds. Amsterdam: North Holland, pp. 99–134.

Woodford, Michael. 2001a. "Inflation Stabilization and Welfare." NBER Working Paper No. 8071. Cambridge, MA: National Bureau of Economic Research.

———. 2001b. "The Taylor Rule and Optimal Monetary Policy." *American Economic Review* 91(2): 232–237.

7

Combining Forecasts with Many Predictors

Tae-Hwy Lee
University of California, Riverside

In practice it is quite common that one forecast model performs well in certain periods while other models perform better in other periods. It is difficult to find a forecast model that outperforms all competing models. To improve forecasts over individual models, combined forecasts have been suggested (Bates and Granger 1969). Researchers including Newbold and Granger (1974), Granger and Newbold (1986, Ch. 9), Granger and Jeon (2004), and Yang (2004) show that forecast combinations can improve forecast accuracy over a single model and show why the forecast combination can achieve a better forecast in terms of mean squared forecast error. Bayesian model averaging may be used to form a weighted combined forecast. (See, e.g., Lee and Yang [2006].) A matter frequently discussed in the literature is how to combine forecasts to achieve the most accurate result. (See Granger and Ramanathan [1984]; Deutsch, Granger, and Teräsvirta [1994]; Palm and Zellner [1992]; Shen and Huang [2006]; and Hansen [2008].) Clemen (1989) and Timmermann (2006) provide excellent surveys on forecast combination and related issues.

Granger and Jeon (2004, p. 327) put the forecast combination in a general context of *thick* modeling and write, "An advantage of thick modeling is that one no longer needs to worry about difficult decisions between close alternatives or between deciding the outcome of a test that is not decisive. In time series such questions are whether the process has a unit root or not, or how many cointegrations are in a vector of a series. For thick models one considers all plausible alternatives and uses the outputs of the various models."

Even when we have a single model, a combination of forecasts can also be formed over a set of training sets. While, in practice, usually

149

we have a single training set, it can be replicated via bootstrap, and the combined forecast trained over the bootstrap-replicated training sets can improve upon the original forecast of the model. This is the idea of boot-strap aggregating (abbreviated as "bagging"), introduced by Breiman (1996).

Huang and Lee (2010) consider the situation in which one wants to predict an economic variable using the information set of many relevant explanatory variables. As Diebold and Pauly (1990, p. 503) point out, "It must be recognized that in many forecasting situations, particularly in real time, pooling of information sets is either impossible or prohibitively costly." Likewise, when models underlying the forecasts remain partially or completely unknown (as is usually the case in practice—for example, with survey forecasts), one would never be informed about the entire information set. Quite often the combination of forecasts is used when the only things available are individual forecasts (for example, in the case of professional forecasters), while the underlying information set and the model used for generating each individual forecast are unknown.

In this chapter we consider how to combine forecasts in a situation where *many* predictors (in other words, a large information set) are available, or in a situation where *many* forecasts are given but models and predictors used for generating each individual forecast are not necessarily known. In each of these situations, we explain how to use factor models. Much of the results presented here are studied in Chan, Stock, and Watson (1999); Hillebrand et al. (2010); Huang and Lee (2010); Stock and Watson (2002); and Tu and Lee (2009).

DATA-RICH ENVIRONMENT

Bernanke and Boivin (2003) emphasize that the use of a large data set is a common practice, such as in the central bank's policymaking analysis. They write, "Research departments throughout the Federal Reserve System monitor and analyze literally thousands of data series from disparate sources . . . Despite this reality of central bank practice, most empirical analyses have been confined to . . . exploit only a limited amount of information. For example, the VAR methodology generally limits the analysis to eight macroeconomic time series or fewer. This disconnect between central bank practice and academic analysis has several costs . . . It thus seems worthwhile to take into account the fact that in practice monetary policy is made in a data-rich environment" (p. 526).

For example, in forecasting stock market volatility, we can use many predictors from many options' implied volatilities. In predicting output growth and inflation, we can use many available economic predictors (Bernanke and Boivin 2003; Hillebrand et al. 2010; Stock and Watson 2002; Tu and Lee 2009; Wright 2009). Ang and Piazzesi (2003); Ang, Piazzesi, and Wei (2006); Bernanke (1990); Hillebrand et al. (2010); and Stock and Watson (1989) use many yields and yield spreads. To predict retail default probability, a retail credit model uses many borrower-specific predictors.

Bernanke and Boivin (2003, p. 525) confirm the merit of the large data set: "[It] explores the feasibility of incorporating richer information sets into the analysis, both positive and normative, of Fed policy making. We employ a factor-model approach . . . that permits the systematic information in large data sets to be summarized by relatively few estimated factors. With this framework, we confirm Stock and Watson's result that the use of large data sets can improve forecast accuracy . . ."

A natural question arises as to how we should use all those vast data in predicting a target of interest. Using large data, there are advantages to accessing rich information and robustifying against structural instability, which plagues low-dimensional forecasting. While we can exploit these advantages, there are also difficulties attached to using large data due to overwhelming information, which may be highly correlated and noisy.

When there are many predictors in columns of the predictor matrix X with the column number N being large, the dimension N needs to be reduced. One way is to select r ($\ll N$) factors of X, and another way is to select r ($\ll N$) columns of X. The former way, known as a factor model, has recently been a popular approach in economic forecasting, because of pioneering work by Stock and Watson (2002), Bai (2003), and Bai and Ng (2002, 2006), who have explored theoretical and empirical analysis of factor models based on principal components. The latter way, known as variable selection, has been widely studied in statistics. The variable selection serves to reduce N by ranking and selecting a subset of X that is most predictive for a forecast target y, through such methods as LASSO (least absolute shrinkage and selection operator) (Tibshirani 1996), least angle regression (Efron et al. 2004), and elastic net (Zou and Hastie 2005), among many other methods.

While the data-rich environment usually refers to the situation where there are many predictors, it also refers to the situation where there are many forecasts provided by many firms, many departments in an organization, many analyses in an investment bank, many different government agents, and so on. In this paper we consider both cases—namely, the data-rich environment with many predictors with N-vector $x_t = (x_{t1}, x_{t2}, ..., x_{tN})'$, and the data-rich environment with many forecasts with N-vector of forecasts $\hat{y}_{t+h} = \left(\hat{y}_{t+h}^{(1)}, \quad \hat{y}_{t+h}^{(2)}, \quad ..., \quad \hat{y}_{t+h}^{(N)} \right)'$. Below we discuss how we form a forecast under these two types of data-rich environment. In both cases the idea is to combine multiple forecasts. Therefore we begin with a review of the literature on combining forecasts.

When multiple forecasts of the same variables are available, it's typically argued that a combination of those forecasts should be used instead of using any single forecast, even if it's a dominant one (e.g., Timmermann 2006). This is because forecast combinations offer diversification gains, and it's almost impossible to identify ex ante a dominant forecast model. The success of the forecast combinations will in turn depend on how well the combination weights are determined. As summarized in Clemen (1989), a simple average (with weights $\frac{1}{N}$) of the multiple forecasts is typically found to be a good forecast combination. However, the equal weights $\frac{1}{N}$ will be very small when N is very large in a data-rich environment, giving little chance for a better model to work dominantly against bad models. Before we deal with the data-rich environment, we first consider a simplest-case scenario, that of $N = 2$.

COMBINING FORECASTS

Bates and Granger (1969) first introduced the idea of combining forecasts. Let us begin with their brief review of what happens when $N = 2$. Let $\hat{y}_t^{(1)}$ and $\hat{y}_t^{(2)}$ be forecasts of y_{t+1} with errors

$$e_{t+1}^{(i)} = y_{t+1} - \hat{y}_t^{(i)}, \qquad i = 1, 2,$$

so that $Ee_{t+1}^{(i)} = 0,$ $\qquad Ee_{t+1}^{(i)2} = \sigma_i^2,$ and $\qquad Ee_{t+1}^{(1)}e_{t+1}^{(2)} = \rho\sigma_1\sigma_2.$

Define a combined forecast with the weight $w \in (-\infty\ \infty)$,

$$\hat{y}_t^{(c)} = w\hat{y}_t^{(1)} + (1-w)\hat{y}_t^{(2)},$$

its forecast error

$$e_{t+1}^{(c)} = y_{t+1} - \hat{y}_t^{(c)} = we_{t+1}^{(1)} + (1-w)e_{t+1}^{(2)},$$

and its expected squared forecast error loss

$$\sigma_c^2(w) = w^2\sigma_1^2 + (1-w)^2\sigma_2^2 + 2w(1-w)\rho\sigma_1\sigma_2.$$

Minimizing the loss, the optimal combining forecast weight is obtained. This expression is minimized for the value of k given by

$$(7.1) \quad w_{opt} = \arg\min\sigma_c^2(w) = \frac{\sigma_2^2 - \rho\sigma_1\sigma_2}{\sigma_1^2 + \sigma_2^2 - 2\rho\sigma_1\sigma_2}.$$

Substitution yields the minimum achievable error variance as

$$\sigma_c^2(w_{opt}) = \frac{\sigma_1^2\sigma_2^2(1-\rho^2)}{\sigma_1^2 + \sigma_2^2 - 2\rho\sigma_1\sigma_2}.$$

Bates and Granger (1969) show that the optimal combined forecast error loss is smaller than the smaller of the two individual forecast error losses:

$$\sigma_c^2(w_{opt}) \leq \min(\sigma_1^2, \sigma_2^2).$$

Thus, a priori, it is reasonable to expect in most practical situations that the best available combined forecast will outperform the better individual forecast. It cannot, in any case, do worse.

This result has been used across various disciplines (e.g., economics, finance, operations research, meteorology, management, computer science, and machine learning) under the names of combining forecast, ensemble predictor, committee of learners, team of forecasts, consensus of learners, mixture of experts, expert system, and others.

WHY COMBINE?

The forecast combination problem is similar to that of minimizing the variance of a portfolio, with the errors from the individual forecasts playing the role of asset returns (Aiolfi and Timmermann 2006). In practice it is quite common that one forecast model performs well in certain periods while other models perform better in other periods. It is difficult to find a forecast model that outperforms all competing models. Forecast combinations can improve forecast accuracy over a single model. Hong and Lee (2003) find that the combined forecasts are generally the best performer for the mean, and sign prediction for the foreign exchange rate changes.

Aiolfi and Timmermann (2006) consider a forecasting strategy that takes the average over the models in the top quartiles or cluster. There is clear evidence that, in general, a strategy of selecting one best (top) model based on past forecasting performance does not work well. This holds true both for linear and nonlinear forecasting methods. This is analogous to portfolio selection in the stock market.

Why do we combine? Aiolfi and Timmermann (2006) answer this way: "Forecast combination entails using information from a typically large set of forecasts and emerges as an attractive strategy when individual forecasting models are misspecified in a way that is unknown to the modeler. Misspecification is likely to be related not simply to functional form (neglected nonlinearity) but also to instability (structural changes) in the joint distribution of forecasts and the target variable. In this situation, the identity of the best forecasting model is likely to change over time and a key question is for how long the relative performance of forecasting models persists" (p. 33).

Aiolfi and Timmermann (2006, pp. 31–32) also write the following:

> Forecasts are of considerable importance to decision makers throughout economics and finance and are routinely used by private enterprises, government institutions and professional econ-

omists. It is therefore not surprising that considerable effort has gone into designing and estimating forecasting models ranging from simple, autoregressive specifications to complicated nonlinear models or models with time-varying parameters. A reason why such a wide range of forecasting models is often considered is that the true data generating process underlying a particular series of interest is unknown. Even the most complicated model is likely to be misspecified and can, at best, provide a reasonable "local" approximation to the target variable.

I would add that this is particularly so in practical forecasting situations in macroeconomics with a large cross section of forecasting models and a short time-series dimension. Aiolfi and Timmermann (2006, p. 32) go on to make a second point about forecasting models:

> Model instability is a source of misspecification that is likely to be particularly relevant in practice, c.f. Stock and Watson (1996). In its presence, it is highly unlikely that a single model will be dominant uniformly across time and the identity of the best local approximation is likely to change over time. If the identity of the best local model is time-varying, it is implausible that a forecasting strategy that, at each point in time, attempts to select the best current model will work well. Most obviously, if (ex-ante) the identity of the best model varies in a purely random way from period to period, it will not be possible to identify this model by considering past forecasting performance across models. Similarly, if a single best model exists but only outperforms other models by a margin that is small relative to random sampling variation, it becomes difficult to identify this model by means of statistical methods based on past performance. Even if the single best model could be identified in this situation, it is conceivable that diversification gains from combining across a set of forecasting models with similar performance will dominate the strategy of only using a single forecasting model.

HOW TO COMBINE?

The optimal combination weights in Equation (7.1) for $N = 2$ may be extended to a general case with a larger N. However, the estimation of the weights from the regression of the form (Equation [7.2]) may suffer from a large estimation error, especially when N is large, and the forecasts may be highly correlated. The following methods have been widely used in applications.

A natural way is to estimate forecast combination weights by least squares regression or, equivalently, by using portfolio variance minimization methods. The usual problem with this estimation method is that, given the sample sizes typically available in practice, the combination weights are often imprecisely estimated. In particular, this is a problem when the number of models is large relative to the length of the time series, so that the covariance matrix of the forecast errors either cannot be estimated or is estimated very imprecisely. The assumption of a stable covariance structure is unlikely to be satisfied in practice, and weights may be time-varying.

A simpler way is to use the equal weights (simple mean). This becomes a common strategy when the models are of similar quality or when their relative performance is unknown or unstable over time. Stock and Watson (1999) use trimmed mean and median to robustify the simple mean–weighted combined forecasts.

Aiolfi and Timmermann (2006) use ranking of the forecasting model and also use clustering. The premise of this approach is that, when combining forecasts from a large cross section of models, it is generally difficult to distinguish between the performance of the top models, but one can tell the difference between the best and worst models. This suggests including a subset of "good" models in the combined forecast. Another popular method is Bayesian model averaging, which is used in many applications, for example, Lee and Yang (2006) and Wright (2009).

The formula for the optimal combination weights in Equation (7.1) for $N = 2$ has an important aspect that has been ignored in many applications in the literature, although it was discussed in Granger and Newbold (1986, Ch. 9) in some length and detail. That is the role of correlation ρ on the forecast combination as studied in Lee, Li, and Huang (2010). Note that the forecast combination need not be convex, and it is permitted that the weights can be any real number, $w \in (-\infty \; \infty)$. Therefore the optimal forecast combination weight w in Equation (7.1) may be negative (< 0) or larger than 1. What does this mean? How does ρ affect the combined forecast? To combine multiple forecasts when these forecasts are highly correlated or close to collinear, the optimal combination places negative weights on the inferior forecasts and larger than 1 on the dominant forecasts, similar to the pairs-trading strategy that profits from the high correlation of the two sock returns. This optimal forecast combination outperforms any individual forecast and explains why an inferior forecast can be included in the combination to improve the forecast. The optimal combination weight has a pattern similar to that of the pairs-trading strategy. Without loss of generality, we assume all the forecasts are one-step-ahead forecasts. The following results can be easily generalized to multistep forecasts. The situation where $w_{opt} < 0$ is interesting. In light of the above condition, it appears that an inferior forecast may still be worth including with negative weight. This happens when $\sigma_2^2 - \rho\sigma_1\sigma_2 < 0$ or $\sigma_2 / \sigma_1 < \rho$—i.e., when ρ is a very large positive value (say, close to 1) and $f_t^{(1)}$ is the inferior forecast, with larger forecast error variance σ_1.

As shown in Granger and Newbold (1986, p. 268), the optimal combining weight w_{opt} can be estimated from

$$(7.2) \quad \hat{w}_t = \frac{\sum_{s=1}^{t}\left(e_s^{(2)2} - e_s^{(1)}e_s^{(2)}\right)}{\sum_{s=1}^{t}\left(e_s^{(1)2} + e_s^{(2)2} - 2e_s^{(1)}e_s^2\right)},$$

which can be obtained from the regression

$$(7.3) \quad e_{t+1}^{(2)} = w\left(e_{t+1}^{(2)} - e_{t+1}^{(1)}\right) + e_{t+1}^{(c)}.$$

However, a common popular recommendation is to ignore ρ. For example, Clemen (1989, p. 562) suggests "to ignore the effect of correlations in calculating combining weights." While the optimal weight $\hat{w}_t$ can be negative or overweighted (larger than 1) depending on the value of ρ, the use of a simpler form obtained with the restriction $\rho = 0$ has been a popular recommendation:

$$\hat{w}_t' = \frac{\sum_{s=1}^{t} e_s^{(2)2}}{\sum_{s=1}^{t}\left(e_s^{(1)2} + e_s^{(2)2}\right)}.$$

Note that, if we ignore ρ, $\hat{w}_t'$ is always constrained on the $(0,1)$ interval (analogous to the short-sale constraint).

When ρ is large and positive, the optimal weight on the inferior forecast can be negative. The forecast combination problem is analogous to that of minimizing the variance of a portfolio, with the forecast errors playing the role of asset returns (Timmermann 2006). Gatev, Goetzmann, and Rouwenhorst (2006) show that "pairs trading" in financial trading strategy profits from the high correlation in the returns. Analogously, the profitability of using the optimal weight is linked to the high correlation ρ in the forecasts. Without loss of generality, let us assume that $\hat{y}_t^{(1)}$ is the inferior forecast, with larger forecast error variance. In combining forecasts, when $\rho \gg 0$, we short the loser (the worse forecast) with $w < 0$ and buy the winner (the better one) with $(1 - w) > 1$. In this case, the use of $\hat{w}_t'$ while ignoring the correlation ρ would be too restrictive.

FORECASTING IN A DATA-RICH ENVIRONMENT

So far, we have looked at the case of $N = 2$. Most of the combining forecast literature has been limited to the case in which N is small. Now we take up the case of combining forecasts when N is large. Consider a kitchen-sink model with all predictors x_t in one large model

$$y_{t+h} = \begin{pmatrix} 1 & x_t' \end{pmatrix} b + u_t \qquad\qquad (t = 1, 2, ..., T)$$

to generate the h-step forecast

$$\hat{y}_{T+h} = \begin{pmatrix} 1 & x_T' \end{pmatrix} \hat{b}_T .$$

However, when N is large, the OLS estimator $\hat{b}_{OLS}$ may not be feasible to compute, and the mean squared forecast error (MSFE) increases with N as $MSFE = E\left(y_{t+h} - \hat{y}_{t+h}\right)^2 = O\left(\dfrac{N}{T}\right)$. A solution to these problems is not to use OLS estimation of the large model but to reduce the dimension N, either by selection of relevant variables for the forecast target to reduce N or by using a factor model to reduce N, or both. The variable selection is to reduce N by ranking variables in X and selecting a subset of X that is most predictive for a forecast target y, through such methods as forward and backward selection, stepwise regression, LASSO (Tibshirani 1996), least angle regression (Efron et al. 2004), elastic net (Zou and Hastie 2005), and so on.

Alternatively, one can combine the large information in x_t *indirectly* through individual forecasts $\hat{y}_{T+1}^{(i)}$ $(i = 1, \ldots, N)$, and then combine the N individual forecasts

$$y_{t+1}^{(1)} = x_{1t}\beta_1 + \varepsilon_{1,t+1}$$

$$\vdots$$

$$y_{t+1}^{(N)} = x_{Nt}\beta_N + \varepsilon_{N,t+1}$$

to form the combined forecast (at time T using the estimated $\hat{\beta}_i$'s)

$$\hat{y}_{T+1}^{(c)} = w_1 \hat{y}_{T+1}^{(1)} + \ldots + w_N \hat{y}_{T+1}^{(N)} \, .$$

Here each partition of the predictor vector x_t need not contain only one predictor at a time but may contain more, and each partition need not be disjointed. In practice, generally the predictor vector x_t may not be observed when only forecasts are available (e.g., in survey forecasts). Therefore, we will consider two types of data-rich environments. The first is where there are N predictors

$$x_t = \left(x_{t1}, x_{t2}, \ldots, x_{tN} \right)' ,$$

and the second is where there are N forecasts, with

$$\hat{y}_{t+h} = \left(\hat{y}_{t+h}^{(1)}, \hat{y}_{t+h}^{(2)}, \ldots, \hat{y}_{t+h}^{(N)} \right)' .$$

In each type of data-rich environment, we use factor models assuming there are latent factors of the predictors x_t or of the forecasts $\hat{y}_{t+h}$.

FORECASTING WITH MANY PREDICTORS

First, let's consider forecasting when there are N predictors $x_t = (x_{t1}, x_{t2}, \dots, x_{tN})'$ and N is large. Following Stock and Watson (2002), we use a factor model that is based on the factors f_t of the predictors x_t:

$$(7.4) \quad x_t = \Lambda f_t + v_t \; ,$$

where Λ is the factor loading. Once the factors have been extracted from the predictors, the forecast of the target can be formed from the regression of

$$(7.5) \quad y_t = f_t \alpha + u_t \; .$$

As noted in Hillebrand et al. (2010) and Tu and Lee (2009), in this approach, the factors are obtained from the marginal model of x_t rather than the joint model of (y_t, x_t). We write the above model in Equations (7.4) and (7.5) as follows:

$$y_t = E\left(y_t \middle| x_t; \theta_1\right) + u_t = f_t \alpha + u_t \qquad (\theta_1 = \alpha),$$

$$x_t = E(x_t; \theta_2) + v_t = \Lambda f_t + v_t \qquad (\theta_2 = f_t, \Lambda).$$

Note that this assures that the joint density

$$D(y_t, x_t; \theta) = D_1\left(y_t \middle| x_t; \theta_1\right) \times D_t\left(x_t; \theta_2\right),$$

where $\left(\theta_1 \; \theta_2\right) \in \Theta_1 \times \Theta_2$ are variation free and we estimate the conditional model (Equation [7.5]) and the marginal model (Equation [7.4]) separately.

FORECASTING WITH MANY FORECASTS

Next, we consider forecasting when there are N forecasts $\hat{y}_{t+h} = \left(\hat{y}_{t+h}^{(1)}, \hat{y}_{t+h}^{(2)}, \dots, \hat{y}_{t+h}^{(N)}\right)'$ and N is large. In this situation, many forecasts are given either from many survey forecasters or from many analysts. There are various organizations that operate as an aggregate or a group, based on many individual analysts who may or may not use the same information sets. Depending on the shared intersections of various information sets used by survey forecasters or analysts, the correlations among the many individual forecasts may be strong. When the number N of individual forecasts is large, we wish to estimate the weights to form the aggregate forecast (a combined forecast). The N individual forecasts may be given with or without the prescription on how they have been generated. We apply principal component analysis on the forecasts to extract factors

$$\hat{y}_{t+h} = \Lambda f_{t+h} + \upsilon_{t+h}$$

and

$$\hat{f}_{t+h} = \hat{\Lambda}' \hat{y}_{t+h}$$

and estimate the following forecasting equation,

$$(7.6) \quad y_{t+h} = \hat{f}'_{t+h} \alpha + u_{t+h} \ ,$$

to form the eventual forecast

$$\hat{y}_{T+h} = \hat{f}'_{T+h} \hat{\alpha}_T \ .$$

From the above calculations, note that the weights to combine many forecasts are

$$\hat{y}_{T+h} = \hat{f}'_{T+h} \hat{\alpha} = \left(\hat{y}'_{T+h} \hat{\Lambda} \right) \hat{a} = \hat{y}'_{T+h} \hat{w} \ ,$$

and therefore the optimal forecast combination weights are

$$\hat{w} := \hat{\Lambda} \hat{\alpha} \ .$$

Hillebrand et al. (2010) and Tu and Lee (2009) consider the above model when each individual forecast $\hat{y}^{(i)}_{t+h}$ is generated by using one predictor $x^{(i)}_t$ at a time. In their applications, the combined forecast with this weight vector $\hat{w} = \hat{\Lambda}\hat{\alpha}$ outperforms the equally weighted combined forecast. However, it is not necessary to know how each individual forecast $\hat{y}_{t+h}^{(i)}$ is generated. In practice, there are various situations where only the forecasts are given to econometricians, without telling about how the forecasts are obtained.

It is generally believed that it is difficult to estimate the forecast combination weights when N is large. Therefore the equal weights $\left(\frac{1}{N}\right)$ have been widely used instead of estimating weights. An exception is Wright (2009), who uses Bayesian model averaging for pseudo out-of-sample prediction of U.S. inflation and finds that it generally gives more accurate forecasts than simple equal-weighted averaging. He uses $N = 107$ predictors. It is often found in the literature that equally weighted combined forecasts are the best. Stock and Watson (2004) call this the "forecast combination puzzle." (See also Timmermann [2006].) Smith and Wallis (2009) explore a possible explanation of the forecast combination puzzle and conclude that it is due to estimation error of the combining weights. However, the empirical results occur when N is not very large. When N is very large, the equal weights $\left(\frac{1}{N}\right)$ put too little weight to good models, especially when $N \to \infty$, and the equal weights can hardly be justified. Note that we can consistently estimate the combining weights $\hat{w} = \hat{\Lambda}\hat{\alpha}$, as long as $\hat{\Lambda}$ and $\hat{\alpha}$ are estimated consistently. Note also that combining forecasts with the weights $\hat{w} = \hat{\Lambda}\hat{\alpha}$ takes the correlation structure among the forecasts $\hat{y}_{t+h}^{(i)}$ into the calculation of the weights, as it is based on the regression in Equation (7.6), just as in the regression in Equation (7.3) to get Equation (7.2).

FURTHER TOPICS IN COMBINING FORECASTS

We have discussed the combining forecasts for one-step-ahead forecasting, for the conditional mean, of continuous random variables. This can be extended to the following three things:

1) multiple-step-ahead forecasts;

2) conditional variance forecasts, conditional quantile forecasts, conditional density forecasts, and conditional interval forecasts; and

3) discrete random variables (categorized data, binary data).

Combining Multistep Forecasting

Lin and Granger (1994) classify the multistep mean forecast methods into five alternative categories. Let's assume the true DGP can be characterized by the following equation:

$$Y_{t+1} = g(Y_t) + \varepsilon_{t+1},$$

where ε_t is a zero-mean, independent, and identically distributed sequence with distribution function Φ.

The optimal one-step forecast using a least square criterion is

$$Y_{t,1} = E\left[Y_{t+1} | Y_{t-j}, j \geq 0\right] = g(Y_{t-1}).$$

When $g(\cdot)$ is known, there should be no problem in generating a one-step-ahead forecast. When $g(\cdot)$ is not known in practice, we can approximate $g(\cdot)$ by a flexible function form such as the polynomial family or the neural network family. However, the multistep forecasts for nonlinear models are much more complicated than the one-step forecast. Consider the simplest $h = 2$ case as an example to illustrate the multistep forecast methods. The optimal two-step-ahead forecast at time t is as follows:

$$
\begin{aligned}
(7.7) \quad Y_{t,2} &= E\left[Y_{t+2} | Y_{t-j}, \quad j \geq 0\right] \\
&= E\left[g(Y_{t+1}) + \varepsilon_{t+2} | Y_{t-j}, \quad j \geq 0\right] \\
&= E\left[g(g(Y_t) + \varepsilon_{t+1}) | Y_{t-j}, \quad j \geq 0\right].
\end{aligned}
$$

Of the five multistep mean forecast methods, there are four possible ways to do multistep forecasts by iterating one-step-ahead forecasts, as is discussed by Brown and Mariano (1989):

1) Naive (or deterministic):

$$Y_{t,2}^n \equiv g\big(g(Y_t)\big),$$

so that the presence of ε_{t+1} is ignored by putting its value at zero. For most nonlinear function $g(\cdot), Y_{t,2}^n$ will be biased, and the direction of the bias depends on whether $g(\cdot)$ is convex or concave, as discussed by Granger and Newbold (1976).

2) Exact (or optimal, or closed form):

$$Y_{t,2}^e \equiv \int_{-\infty}^{\infty} g\big(g(Y_t) + \varepsilon_{t+1}\big) d\Phi .$$

3) Monte Carlo:

$$Y_{t,2}^m \equiv \frac{1}{J} \sum_{j=1}^{J} g\big(g(Y_t) + \varepsilon_j\big),$$

where $\varepsilon_j = 1, \ldots, J$ are random numbers drawn from the distribution Φ. If J is large enough, $Y_{t,h}^m$ and $Y_{t,h}^e$ should be virtually identical.

4) Bootstrap (or residual-based):

$$Y_{t,2}^b \equiv \frac{1}{t} \sum_{j=1}^{t} g\big(g(Y_t) + \hat{\varepsilon}_j\big),$$

where $\hat{\varepsilon}_j$, $j = 1, \ldots, t$ are the t values of the residual estimated over the sample period.

An alternative way of doing a multistep mean forecast is to model the relationship between Y_{t+h} and Y_t directly by a new function $g_h(\cdot)$:

5) $Y_{t+h} = g_h(Y_t) + e_{t,h}$,

though $e_{t,h}$ is usually not white noise, as mentioned by Lin and Granger (1994). Therefore, a fifth method for doing a multistep forecast is

$$Y_{t,h}^d \equiv g_h(Y_t) .$$

With any of these five methods, the factor models considered in the previous sections may be used for multistep forecasts when there are many predictors or many forecasts.

Combining Quantile Forecasts

The optimal forecast $\hat{y}_{t+1}$ may be estimated, for a given $\alpha \in (0,1)$, from minimizing the check loss:

$$\min_{\hat{y}_{t+1}} \rho_\alpha \left(e_{t+1} \right) = \left[\alpha - 1 \left(e_{t+1} < 0 \right) \right] \times e_{t+1} ,$$

where $e_{t+1} = y_{t+1} - \hat{y}_{t+1}$. Since $\rho_\alpha(\cdot)$ is convex, the results of Bates and Granger (1969), as discussed in the next section, can be carried over.

Note that the optimal forecast $\hat{y}_{t+1}^* = q_\alpha \left(y_{t+1} | x_t \right)$ satisfies the following first-order condition:

$$E \left(\alpha - 1 \left(y_{t+1} < \hat{y}_{t+1}^* \right) | x_t \right) = 0 , \qquad \text{a.s.}$$

(See, e.g., Giacomini and Komunjer [2005].) Hence,

$$g_{t+1} \equiv \alpha - 1 \left(y_{t+1} < \hat{y}_{t+1}^* \right)$$

may be called the generalized residual or generalized forecast error. From this we obtain

$$\alpha = E \left(1 \left(y_{t+1} < \hat{y}_{t+1}^* \right) | x_t \right) = Pr \left(y_{t+1} \le \hat{y}_{t+1}^* | x_t \right).$$

It is interesting to note that this corresponds exactly to Equation (7.8) on page 169 for evaluating interval forecasts, whereas here we apply it to the optimal forecast $\hat{y}_{t+1}^*$.

We consider two types of data-rich environments—one where there are N predictors,

$$x_t = \left(x_{t1}, x_{t2}, \ldots, x_{tN} \right)' ,$$

and another where there are N quantile forecasts, with

$$\hat{y}_{t+h} = \left(\hat{y}_{t+h}^{(1)}, \hat{y}_{t+h}^{(2)}, \ldots, \hat{y}_{t+h}^{(N)} \right)' .$$

It is necessary to generalize the principal component regression for conditional quantiles under the check loss $\rho_\alpha(\cdot)$.

Combining Density Forecasts

Suppose that $\{y_t\}_{t=-\infty}^{\infty}$ is a time series (e.g., the return of a portfolio over a certain period) with unknown conditional density function $f_t(y) \equiv f_t(y|x_{t-1})$. Let $p_t(y,\theta) \equiv p_t(y|x_{t-1},\theta)$ be a one-step-ahead conditional density forecast model, where θ is a finite-dimensional parameter. Suppose that $p_t(y,\theta_0) = f_t(y)$ for some θ_0. Then, show that the one-step-ahead density forecast is optimal in the sense that it dominates all other density forecasts for any loss function (Diebold, Gunther, and Tay 1998; Granger 1999; Granger and Pesaran 2000). In practice it is not uncommon that a suboptimal forecast model does better than another in predicting a certain aspect of the distribution (e.g., value at risk at the 5 percent level) but worse than another in predicting a different aspect of the distribution (e.g., value at risk at the 1 percent level). This makes it difficult for forecast users (who may not be forecast producers) to choose a suitable forecast model. The fact that the optimal forecast model is preferred by all forecast users regardless of their loss functions resolves this difficulty. It is therefore useful to check whether a density forecast model is optimal, and, if not, to determine what useful information can be provided from it for further improvement in density forecasts. In fact, even if point forecasts are of interest, the optimal conditional density forecasts are needed to construct optimal point forecasts under a general asymmetric loss function (Christoffersen and Diebold 1996, 1997).

Suppose that $\{y_t\}$ is generated from conditional densities $\{f_t(y)\}$. If a sequence of density forecasts $\{p_t(y,\theta_0)\}$ coincides with $\{f_t(y)\}$, then under the usual condition of a nonzero Jacobian with continuous partial derivatives, $\{Z_t\}$ is IID $U[0,1]$. That is, when the forecast model $p_t(y,\theta)$ is optimal, the series of PITs, $\{Z_t\}$, where

$$Z_t \equiv \int_{-\infty}^{y_t} p_t(y,\theta_0)\,dy,$$

is IID $U[0,1]$. (See Diebold, Gunther and Tay [1998].) Berkowitz (2001) considers the inverse normal transformation of the PIT, which follows IID $N(0,1)$. Bao, Lee, and Saltoglu (2007) discuss how the Kullback-

Leibler Information Criterion (KLIC) of Kullback and Leibler (1951), based on PIT, may be used to compare the density forecasts. (See Mitchell and Hall [2005] for combining density forecasts.) Combining many density forecasts (with large N),

$$\left(\hat{f}_{t+h}^{(1)}(y), \hat{f}_{t+h}^{(2)}(y), \ldots, \hat{f}_{t+h}^{(N)}(y) \right)',$$

would require combinations of conditional moments or conditional quantiles, with mixtures of several distributions, which would be complicated.

Combining Interval Forecasts

Consider a stationary series $\{y_t\}_{t=1}^{T}$. Let the one-period-ahead conditional interval forecast made at time t from a model be denoted as

$$J_{t,1}(\alpha) = \left(L_{t,1}(\alpha), U_{t,1}(\alpha) \right), \qquad t = R, \ldots, T,$$

where $L_{t,1}(\alpha)$ and $U_{t,1}(\alpha)$ are the lower and upper limits of the ex ante interval forecast for time $t+1$ made at time t with the coverage probability α, i.e., $\alpha = Pr[y_{t+1} \in J_{t,1}(\alpha)|x_t]$. If we define the indicator variable as $d_{t+1}(\alpha) = \mathbf{1}[y_{t+1} \in J_{t,1}(\alpha)]$, the sequence $\{d_{t+1}(\alpha)\}_{t=R}^{T}$ is IID Bernoulli (α). The optimal interval forecast would satisfy

(7.8) $E\left(d_{t+1}(\alpha)|x_t\right) = \alpha$,

so that $\{d_{t+1}(\alpha) - \alpha\}$ will be a martingale difference sequence. As the $\{d_{t+1}(\alpha)\}$ has the expected Bernoulli log-likelihood

$$E\alpha^{d_{t+1}(\alpha)} (1-\alpha)^{[1-d_{t+1}(\alpha)]},$$

we can choose a model with the largest out-of-sample mean of

$$p^{-1} \sum_{t=R}^{T} \log \left(\alpha^{\hat{d}_{t+1}(\alpha)} [1-\alpha]^{[1-\hat{d}_{t+1}(\alpha)]} \right).$$

(See Bao, Lee, and Saltoglu [2006].)

To combine interval forecasts that are generated from multiple models, one can use the conditional quantile forecasts derived from using regression quantiles for $L_{t,1}(\alpha)$ and $U_{t,1}(\alpha)$ and combine them; or one can use the conditional density forecasts, combine them, and invert the combined density forecast to get the conditional quantile forecasts for $L_{t,1}(\alpha)$ and $U_{t,1}(\alpha)$, using the methods discussed in Section 9.2.

Combining Binary Forecasts

Lee and Yang (2006) consider binary forecasts using bagging to form a (weighted) average over all bootstrap training samples drawn from the same distribution. The idea can be extended to cases where there are many predictors or many forecasts to form a combined forecast of many binary forecasts. As in Lee and Yang, the combined binary predictor $\hat{y}_t^{(c)}$ can be constructed by the majority voting on the N individual binary forecasts $\hat{y}_t^{(i)}$ ($i = 1, \ldots, N$), i.e.,

$$\hat{y}_t^{(c)} = 1\left(\sum_{i=1}^{N} w_i \hat{y}_t^{(i)} > \frac{1}{2} \right),$$

where $\sum_{i=1}^{N} w_i = 1$. It is not clear how to estimate the combination weights $\{w_i\}$ when N is large. Simple cases are those where we assume a perfect democracy, with $w_i = \frac{1}{N}$ for all i, and those where we assume a dictator, with $w_i = 1$ for some i. Neither case can be optimal in terms of the binary loss functions.

CONCLUSIONS

We have considered how to combine forecasts in a data-rich environment with many predictors, $x_t = \left(x_{t1}, x_{t2}, \ldots, x_{tN} \right)'$, or with many forecasts, $\hat{y}_{t+h} = \left(\hat{y}_{t+h}^{(1)}, \hat{y}_{t+h}^{(2)}, \ldots, \hat{y}_{t+h}^{(N)} \right)$ (when N is large). In practice there are situations where we, whether econometricians or forecasters, do not observe the predictors but only the forecasts (e.g., survey forecasts of the Federal Reserve Bank of Philadelphia). In such situations one needs to aggregate many forecasts into a consensus group forecast. A common way is to use the simple average, or majority voting. While many empirical results from out-of-sample forecasting have shown that the simple average of multiple forecasts tends to work well, such a conclusion assumes that all individual forecasts are equally good by assigning equal weights. The accuracy can be improved if the weights can be estimated consistently without experiencing errors from the usual large N problem (the so-called curse of dimensionality). We use a factor model of many forecasts to derive the forecast combination weights without succumbing to this problem.

In a data-rich environment with many predictors or many forecasts, it is often necessary to use reduced-dimension specifications that can span a large number of predictors. In the recent forecasting literature, the use of factor models and principal component estimation has been advocated for forecasting in the presence of many predictors. In this situation, we decompose the space spanned by many predictors using the principal components, as in Stock and Watson (2002). We can also project the forecast target to many subspaces spanned by the predictors, obtain many artificially generated forecasts, and then combine those forecasts generated from the subspaces, as in Chan, Stock, and Watson (1999); Hillebrand et al. (2010); and Tu and Lee (2009).

References

Aiolfi, Marco, and Alan Timmermann. 2006. "Persistence in Forecasting Performance and Conditional Combination Strategies." *Journal of Econometrics* 135(1–2): 31–53.

Ang, Andrew, and Monika Piazzesi. 2003. "A No-Arbitrage Vector Autoregression of Term Structure Dynamics with Macroeconomic and Latent Variables." *Journal of Monetary Economics* 50(4): 745–787.

Ang, Andrew, Monika Piazzesi, and Min Wei. 2006. "What Does the Yield Curve Tell Us about GDP Growth?" *Journal of Econometrics* 131(1–2): 359–403.

Bai, Jushan. 2003. "Inferential Theory for Factor Models of Large Dimensions." *Econometrica* 71(1): 135–171.

Bai, Jushan, and Serena Ng. 2002. "Determining the Number of Factors in Approximate Factor Models." *Econometrica* 70(1): 191–221.

———. 2006. "Confidence Intervals for Diffusion Index Forecasts and Inference for Factor-Augmented Regressions." *Econometrica* 74(4): 1133–1150.

Bao, Yong, Tae-Hwy Lee, and Burak Saltoglu. 2006. "Evaluating Predictive

Performance of Value-at-Risk Models in Emerging Markets: A Reality Check." *Journal of Forecasting* 25(2): 101–128.

———. 2007. "Comparing Density Forecast Models." *Journal of Forecasting* 26(3): 203–225.

Bates, J.M., and Clive W.J. Granger. 1969. "The Combination of Forecasts." *Operational Research Quarterly* 20(4): 451–468.

Berkowitz, Jeremy. 2001. "Testing Density Forecasts, with Applications to Risk Management." *Journal of Business and Economic Statistics* 19(4): 465–474.

Bernanke, Ben S. 1990. "On the Predictive Power of Interest Rates and Interest Rate Spreads." Federal Reserve Bank of Boston's *New England Economic Review* 1990(November/December): 51–68.

Bernanke, Ben S., and Jean Boivin. 2003. "Monetary Policy in a Data-Rich Environment." *Journal of Monetary Economics* 50(3): 525–546.

Breiman, Leo. 1996. "Bagging Predictors." *Machine Learning* 24(2): 123–140.

Brown, Bryan W., and Roberto S. Mariano. 1989. "Predictors in Dynamic Nonlinear Models: Large-Sample Behavior." *Econometric Theory* 5(3): 430–452.

Chan, Yeung Lewis, James H. Stock, and Mark W. Watson. 1999. "A Dynamic Factor Model Framework for Forecast Combination." *Spanish Economic Review* 1(2): 91–121.

Christoffersen, Peter F., and Francis X. Diebold. 1996. "Further Results on Forecasting and Model Selection under Asymmetric Loss." *Journal of Applied Econometrics* 11(5): 561–572.

———. 1997. "Optimal Prediction under Asymmetric Loss." *Econometric Theory* 13(6): 808–817.

Clemen, Robert T. 1989. "Combining Forecasts: A Review and Annotated Bibliography." *International Journal of Forecasting* 5(4): 559–583.

Deutsch, Melinda, Clive W.J. Granger, and Timo Teräsvirta. 1994. "The Combination of Forecasts Using Changing Weights." *International Journal of Forecasting* 10(1): 47–57.

Diebold, Francis X., Todd A. Gunther, and Anthony S. Tay. 1998. "Evaluating Density Forecasts with Applications to Financial Risk Management." *International Economic Review* 39(4): 863–883.

Diebold, Francis X., and Peter Pauly. 1990. "The Use of Prior Information in Forecast Combination." *International Journal of Forecasting* 6(4): 503–508.

Efron, Bradley, Trevor Hastie, Iain Johnstone, and Robert Tibshirani. 2004. "Least Angle Regression." With discussion. *Annals of Statistics* 32(2): 407–499.

Gatev, Evan, William N. Goetzmann, and K.Geert Rouwenhorst. 2006. "Pairs

Trading: Performance of a Relative-Value Arbitrage Rule." *Review of Financial Studies* 19(3): 797–827.

Giacomini, Raffaella, and Ivana Komunjer. 2005. "Evaluation and Combination of Conditional Quantile Forecasts." *Journal of Business and Economic Statistics* 23(4): 416–431.

Granger, Clive W.J. 1999. *Empirical Modeling in Economics: Specification and Evaluation*. Cambridge: Cambridge University Press.

Granger, Clive W.J., and Yongil Jeon. 2004. "Thick Modelling." *Economic Modelling* 21(2): 323–343.

Granger, Clive W.J., and Paul Newbold. 1976. "Forecasting Transformed Series." *Journal of the Royal Statistical Society* B 38(2): 189–203.

———. 1986. *Forecasting Economic Time Series,* 2d ed. New York: Academic Press.

Granger, Clive W.J., and M. Hashem Pesaran. 2000. "Economic and Statistical Measures of Forecast Accuracy." *Journal of Forecasting* 19(7): 537–560.

Granger, Clive W.J., and Ramu Ramanathan. 1984. "Improved Methods of Combining Forecasts." *Journal of Forecasting* 3(2): 197–204.

Hansen, Bruce E. 2008. "Least-Squares Forecast Averaging." *Journal of Econometrics* 146(2): 342–350.

Hillebrand, Eric, Tae-Hwy Lee, Canlin Li, and Huiyu Huang. 2010. "Forecasting Output Growth and Inflation: How to Use Information in the Yield Curve." Working paper. Riverside, CA: University of California, Riverside.

Hong, Yongmiao, and Tae-Hwy Lee. 2003. "Inference on Predictability of Foreign Exchange Rates via Generalized Spectrum and Nonlinear Time Series Models." *Review of Economics and Statistics* 85(4): 1048–1062.

Huang, Huiyu, and Tae-Hwy Lee. 2010. "To Combine Forecasts or to Combine Information?" *Econometric Reviews* 29(5–6): 534–570.

Kullback, S., and R.A. Leibler. 1951. "On Information and Sufficiency." *Annals of Mathematical Statistics* 22(1): 79–86.

Lee, Tae-Hwy, Canlin Li, and Huiyu Huang. 2010. "Pairs Trading Strategy for Combining Forecasts." Working paper. Riverside, CA: University of California, Riverside.

Lee, Tae-Hwy, and Yang Yang. 2006. "Bagging Binary and Quantile Predictors for Time Series." *Journal of Econometrics* 135(1–2): 465–497.

Lin, Jin-Lung, and Clive W.J. Granger. 1994. "Forecasting from Non-Linear Models in Practice." *Journal of Forecasting* 13(1): 1–9.

Mitchell, James, and Stephen G. Hall. 2005. "Evaluating, Comparing, and Combining Density Forecasts Using the KLIC with an Application to the Bank of England and NIESR 'Fan' Charts of Inflation." *Oxford Bulletin of Economics and Statistics* 67(S1): 995–1033.

Newbold, Paul, and Clive W.J. Granger. 1974. "Experience with Forecasting Univariate Time Series and the Combination of Forecasts." *Journal of the Royal Statistical Society* 137(2): 131–165.

Palm, Franz C., and Arnold Zellner. 1992. "To Combine or Not to Combine? Issues of Combining Forecasts." *Journal of Forecasting* 11(8): 687–701.

Shen, Xiaotong, and Hsin-Cheng Huang. 2006. "Optimal Model Assessment, Selection, and Combination." *Journal of the American Statistical Association* 101(474): 554–568.

Smith, Jeremy, and Kenneth F. Wallis. 2009. "A Simple Explanation of the Forecast Combination Puzzle." *Oxford Bulletin of Economics and Statistics* 71(3): 331–355.

Stock, James H., and Mark W. Watson. 1989. "New Indexes of Coincident and Leading Economic Indicators." In *NBER Macroeconomics Annual 1989*, Vol. 4, Olivier Jean Blanchard and Stanley Fischer, eds. Cambridge, MA: MIT Press, pp. 351–408.

———. 1996. "Evidence on Structural Instability in Macroeconomic Time Series Relations." *Journal of Business and Economic Statistics* 14(1): 11–30.

———. 1999. "A Comparison of Linear and Nonlinear Univariate Models for Forecasting Macroeconomic Time Series." In *Cointegration, Causality, and Forecasting: A Festschrift in Honour of Clive W.J. Granger*, Robert F. Engle and Halbert White, eds. Oxford: Oxford University Press, pp. 1–45.

———. 2002. "Forecasting Using Principal Components from a Large Number of Predictors." *Journal of the American Statistical Association* 97(460): 1167–1179.

———. 2004. "Combination Forecasts of Output Growth in a Seven-Country Data Set." *Journal of Forecasting* 23(6): 405–430.

Tibshirani, Robert. 1996. "Regression Shrinkage and Selection via the Lasso." *Journal of the Royal Statistical Society*, Series B, 58(1): 267–288.

Timmermann, Allan. 2006. "Forecast Combinations." In *Handbook of Economic Forecasting*, Vol. 1, Graham Elliott, Clive W.J. Granger, and Allan Timmermann, eds. Amsterdam: North-Holland, pp. 135–196.

Tu, Yundong, and Tae-Hwy Lee. 2009. "Forecasting Using Supervised Factor Models." Working paper. Riverside, CA: University of California, Riverside.

Wright, Jonathan H. 2009. "Forecasting U.S. Inflation by Bayesian Model Averaging." *Journal of Forecasting* 28(2): 131–144.

Yang, Yuhong. 2004. "Combining Forecasting Procedures: Some Theoretical Results." *Econometric Theory* 20(1): 176–222.

Zou, Hui, and Trevor Hastie. 2005. "Regularization and Variable Selection via the Elastic Net." *Journal of the Royal Statistical Society* B 67(2): 301–320.

Authors

Michael D. Bradley is a professor of economics at George Washington University. His primary areas of research are the conduct and effects of monetary policy, the economics of postal and delivery services, and the application of nonlinear models to issues in macroeconomics and finance. He has published over 50 papers in academic journals and scholarly books and has won a number of awards for his academic work, including the Richard D. Irwin Distinguished Paper Award and the Trachtenberg Prize for Excellence in Teaching. He earned his PhD from the University of North Carolina at Chapel Hill.

Dean Croushore is a professor of economics and a Rigsby Fellow at the University of Richmond and serves as chair of the economics department. He came to the University of Richmond in 2003 after having spent 14 years as an economist at the Federal Reserve Bank of Philadelphia. He earned his doctorate at Ohio State University. Dr. Croushore is the author of the money and banking textbook *M&B*, published by Cengage Learning, and is coauthor with Andrew Abel and Ben Bernanke of *Macroeconomics*, 7th edition. He is currently a visiting scholar at the Federal Reserve Bank of Philadelphia's Real-Time Data Research Center.

Matthew L. Higgins is an associate professor of economics at Western Michigan University. His areas of research interest are econometric theory, time series analysis, and forecasting. The author of numerous articles in journals including *Applied Economics*, the *Journal of Business and Economic Statistics*, the *Journal of Quantitative Economics*, and the *Journal of Time Series Analysis*, he has written extensively on the theory of empirical models for asset price volatility. He earned his PhD from the University of Illinois.

Dennis W. Jansen is a professor of economics at Texas A&M University. He received his PhD from the University of North Carolina at Chapel Hill. Dr. Jansen's research includes work on forecasting, monetary policy, financial economics and portfolio selection, applied econometrics, and the economics of education. He is affiliated with and is Jordan Professor of Public Policy at the Private Enterprise Research Center, also at Texas A&M University.

Kajal Lahiri is a distinguished professor of economics at the University at Albany, State University of New York, a fellow of CESifo Research Network, and an honorary fellow of the International Institute of Forecasters. He received his doctorate in economics from the University of Rochester. The author of numerous books and articles, Dr. Lahiri created the Transportation Services Index, a measure of output in the transportation sector that is reported monthly by the U.S. Department of Transportation. He is on the editorial boards of the *Journal of Econometrics*, the *International Journal of Forecasting, Empirical Economics*, and the *Journal of Business Cycle Measurement and Analysis*. His current research deals with economic forecasting, and also with minority health—the latter research is being funded by the National Institutes of Health.

Tae-Hwy Lee is a professor of economics at the University of California, Riverside. His research areas are econometrics and its applications to financial and macroeconomic time series for various methodological and empirical issues in specification, testing, estimation, and forecasting. His publications have appeared in the *Journal of Econometrics, Econometric Theory*, the *Journal of Applied Econometrics*, the *Review of Economics and Statistics*, and many other scholarly publications. He earned a PhD in economics from the University of California, San Diego.

David E. Rapach is an associate professor of economics and a research fellow at the Simon Center for Regional Forecasting at Saint Louis University. His research interests include applied time series econometrics, forecasting, macroeconomics, monetary economics, international finance, and financial economics. He has published in numerous journals, including the *Review of Financial Studies*, the *Journal of Portfolio Management*, the *Journal of International Money and Finance*, and the *International Journal of Forecasting*. He is also coeditor of *Forecasting in the Presence of Structural Breaks and Model Uncertainty*, published in 2008 by Emerald Group. He obtained his doctorate in economics from American University.

Herman O. Stekler is a research professor at George Washington University. He has been interested in forecasting issues since 1959, with a special emphasis on forecast evaluations. He has published articles in both economics and forecasting journals. He earned his doctorate from the Massachusetts Institute of Technology.

Index

The italic letters *f, n,* and *t* following a page number indicate that the subject information of the heading is within a figure, note, or table, respectively, on that page. Double italics indicate multiple but consecutive elements.

ADF (Augmented Dickey-Fuller) test, 76–77, 77*t*
Age, long-term forecast evaluation and employment by, 5, 127, 128*t*–129*t*, 130, 143*t*
ALFRED database, 12, 24*n*3
Allison, Robert, 8
American Statistical Association, 8
AR (autoregressive) models. *See* Autoregressive models
ARDL models. *See* Autoregressive distributed lag models
ARIMA model, 109, 122–123
ARMA model. *See* Autoregressive moving average model
Asset prices forecasting with nonlinear models, 1, 4, 62*n*9, 65–102
data description of key variables, 69–72, 70*f*, 71*f*, 72*f*
estimating the linear models, 76–81, 77*t*, 78*t*, 81*t*
estimating the nonlinear models, 73–76, 76*f*, 82–92, 83*t*, 84*t*, 85*f*, 86*t*, 87*f*, 88*ff*, 89*ff*, 90*f*, 91*tt*
forecast evaluation, 92–99, 93*t*, 94*f*, 95*f*, 96*f*, 98*t*, 99*t*
multiple-step-ahead forecasting, 100–102
nonlinear characteristics, 65–67
theoretical preliminaries, 68–69
Augmented Dickey-Fuller (ADF) test, 76–77, 77*t*
Austria, 45
year(s)-ahead forecasts for, 29*t*, 30*f*, 32
Autoregressive (AR) model, 4, 18, 55
as benchmark, 32–33, 34, 47*n*2, 60–61, 61*t*
outperformance of, 56–57, 58, 59

See also Smooth transition autoregressive (STAR) model; Threshold autoregressive (TAR) model
Autoregressive distributed lag (ARDL) model
forecast combination and, 55–56
specific, and state-level employment growth, 60, 61*t*
Autoregressive moving average (ARMA) model, benchmark revisions and, 18

Bagging methodology. *See* Bootstrap aggregating
Bank of England, forecast error and, 25
Bayesian model averaging (BMA), weighted combined forecasts and, 149, 162
Beige Book, monetary policy and, 51
Belgium, 45
year(s)-ahead forecasts for, 29*t*, 30*f*
Benchmarks, 18, 137*n*18
AR models as, 32–33, 34, 47*n*2, 60–61, 61*t*
comparing forecasters and, 109–110
population and, 132, 133*f*, 137*n*27
unemployment and, 125, 137*n*25
Bias test in accurate forecasting, 58, 124, 135*n*4
errors and, 117, 120
unbiasedness definition, 9, 45, 108–109
Binary forecasts, 6, 168
BLS. *See* U.S. Bureau of Labor Statistics
Blue Chip Forecasters (firm), 108
BMA (Bayesian model averaging), 149, 162
Bootstrap aggregating, 3, 54–55, 102, 150, 168

About the Institute

The W.E. Upjohn Institute for Employment Research is a nonprofit research organization devoted to finding and promoting solutions to employment-related problems at the national, state, and local levels. It is an activity of the W.E. Upjohn Unemployment Trustee Corporation, which was established in 1932 to administer a fund set aside by Dr. W.E. Upjohn, founder of The Upjohn Company, to seek ways to counteract the loss of employment income during economic downturns.

The Institute is funded largely by income from the W.E. Upjohn Unemployment Trust, supplemented by outside grants, contracts, and sales of publications. Activities of the Institute comprise the following elements: 1) a research program conducted by a resident staff of professional social scientists; 2) a competitive grant program, which expands and complements the internal research program by providing financial support to researchers outside the Institute; 3) a publications program, which provides the major vehicle for disseminating the research of staff and grantees, as well as other selected works in the field; and 4) an Employment Management Services division, which manages most of the publicly funded employment and training programs in the local area.

The broad objectives of the Institute's research, grant, and publication programs are to 1) promote scholarship and experimentation on issues of public and private employment and unemployment policy, and 2) make knowledge and scholarship relevant and useful to policymakers in their pursuit of solutions to employment and unemployment problems.

Current areas of concentration for these programs include causes, consequences, and measures to alleviate unemployment; social insurance and income maintenance programs; compensation; workforce quality; work arrangements; family labor issues; labor-management relations; and regional economic development and local labor markets.